Dolforwyn C...
Montgomery Castle

Lawrence Butler MA, PhD, FSA, MIFA
and Jeremy K. Knight BA, FSA

A History of the Castles

Introduction

Near the quiet, picturesque town of Montgomery, on the border between England and Wales, the Severn valley broadens as it leaves the Welsh hills and enters the English Midland plain. Hereabouts, the valley forms a natural route into the heart of Wales and the bottleneck created where it narrows, together with an important river crossing at the ford of Rhyd Chwima (Rhyd Whyman), make the area around Montgomery a strategic keypoint on the Welsh March.

To Bishop Rowland Lee (d. 1543), Henry VIII's President of the Council in Wales and the Marches, Montgomery Castle was 'the second key of Wales' — the first being Ludlow. This strategic importance is marked by the ancient fortifications found within a few miles' radius of the present town. The Iron Age hillfort of Ffridd Faldwyn, whose origins date from Neolithic times, stands on the hill adjacent to the castle. Forden Gaer, the second largest Roman auxiliary fort in Wales, occupied until late Roman times, is 1.5 miles (2.5km) away, close to Rhyd Chwima. Offa's Dyke, the eighth-century frontier earthwork built by King Offa of Mercia (757–96) to demarcate his border with the rulers of Wales is visible, just half a mile (0.8km) from the castle. And at Chirbury, some 3 miles (5km) east of Montgomery, Aethelflaed, lady of the Saxon kingdom of Mercia, built a *burh* or fortress in 915 to protect this vulnerable sector of the border with Wales.

The Normans, too, arrived in the area and within ten years of the Conquest had built an earth-and-timber castle close to Rhyd Chwima. From here they could make exploratory incursions into Wales; they could also retreat here as the pendulum of power swung to and fro across the border. Gradually, great independent lordships subject to their own laws were carved out in the borderlands between England and Wales — or the March as it became known.

The resulting tensions ensured that the area around Montgomery would continue to be disputed between Welsh princes, English kings and Marcher barons for the next two centuries.

But it was in the thirteenth century that the area became the scene for some of the most significant events in the history of Wales. By 1218, Llywelyn ab Iorwerth, prince of Gwynedd (d. 1240), held sway over most of native Wales, and included in his custody southern Powys and Montgomery. From here he could invade England as well as secure the route between Gwynedd and south Wales. Llywelyn was clearly a threat to king and Marcher lord alike, so much so that in 1223 King Henry III (1216–72) mounted a punitive expedition culminating in the construction of a brand new stone-built castle at Montgomery to protect the area, now under royal control.

The strategic importance of Rhyd Chwima has already been alluded to, but its political significance intensified as it became a customary meeting place for the representatives of the kings of England and princes of Wales. It was here, in 1267, close to the newly built royal castle at Montgomery, that Henry III formally acknowledged Llywelyn's grandson, Llywelyn ap Gruffudd, prince of Wales (d. 1282). As prince of Wales Llywelyn was determined not only to protect his newly recognized principality but also to display his position in a manner appropriate to his status.

A coin of Offa (757–96), the Anglo-Saxon king of Mercia who raised the great earthwork frontier that demarcated his border with the kingdoms of the Welsh. Offa's Dyke lies just half a mile east of Montgomery (National Museums & Galleries of Wales).

Opposite: The area around Montgomery has long been of strategic importance for the security of the border between England and Wales. Perched high on a rocky outcrop, the thirteenth-century castle overlooks the Severn valley — the main route into Wales from the Midlands. The Iron Age hillfort of Ffridd Faldwyn is on the wooded hill to the right of the castle and Offa's Dyke is in the foreground.

Left: Close to modern Montgomery and near Rhyd Chwima, the important ford across the river Severn, the Normans built an earth-and-timber castle of a type similar to that shown in this illustration from the Bayeux Tapestry (City of Bayeux).

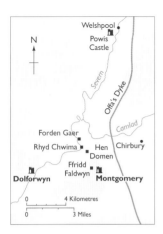

A map showing the sites of strategic importance in the vicinity of Montgomery that are mentioned in the text.

Just six years later, he began to build an impressive stone fortress high above the river Severn at Dolforwyn, close to Abermule, and just 4 miles (6.5km) from Montgomery. The proximity of two such castles, and the opposing aspirations of the Welsh prince and the English king, almost inevitably led to tensions that ultimately precipitated the conquest of Wales by King Edward I (1272–1307) between 1277 and 1283 and the death of Llywelyn in 1282.

Thereafter, Montgomery was held principally by the powerful Marcher family, the Mortimers of Wigmore, Herefordshire, and by the Herbert family, until its destruction in the seventeenth century; Dolforwyn also passed to the Mortimers. But neither castle was to occupy the national stage again and gradually they fell into decay and ruin. Fortunately, both castles fared better during the course of the twentieth century when they were given into State care and following painstaking excavation Dolforwyn and Montgomery are now on public display. Together, they offer a unique opportunity to compare the building methods of the Welsh princes with those of the kings of England and to explore a critical period in the history of Wales.

Montgomery before Montgomery Castle

Just five years after the battle of Hastings (1066), Roger of Montgomery (d. 1094), from St Germain de Montgommeri in Calvados, Normandy, was installed at Shrewsbury and created earl of the same name by King William I (1066–87). He was one of three close supporters of the king, endowed with almost regal powers to protect the frontier with Wales. As part of the process of conquest and consolidation, *Domesday Book* records that Earl Roger built a castle named Montgomery — presumably after his ancestral home — and it was from here that the land-hungry Normans sought to extend their territory along the Severn valley into central Wales and beyond. The Welsh chronicle, *Brut y Tywysogyon*, records that 'the French ravaged

Ceredigion and Dyfed' in 1073–74 and again in 1093–94 when Earl Roger and his son, Arnulf, succeeded in establishing a military outpost at Dingeraint, the forerunner of Cardigan. Closer to home, Earl Roger's forces had swept through the Severn valley, establishing a string of motte-and-bailey castles from Montgomery to Moat Lane, near Llandinam, from where he managed to impose a measure of overlordship on the surrounding Welsh districts.

The Welsh, however, began to retaliate and in 1095 Montgomery was attacked by Cadwgan ap Bleddyn, prince of Powys (d. 1111), precipitating an ineffective royal military campaign by the new king, William Rufus (1087–1100). In 1098, Montgomery passed to Roger's elder son, Robert of Bellême (d. 1131), but in 1102 he was stripped of his lands for his part in a rebellion against Henry I (1100–35). With Robert in exile, the power and influence of the Montgomery family came to an abrupt end. The king exploited the situation and retained most of the forfeited lands, but entrusted Montgomery to the altogether less powerful Baldwin de Boulers and it is probably from him, or his grandson, another Baldwin, that Montgomery derives its Welsh name Trefaldwyn — 'Baldwin's town'.

At this time, however, Montgomery was not the town and castle that we see today, but the earth-and-timber motte-and-bailey castle of Hen Domen, erected close to Rhyd Chwima, 1 mile (1.6km) distant from the site of the present castle. Hen Domen's timber defences and buildings have been revealed through careful excavation, and until the foundation of the present castle and town in 1223 references to Montgomery were to the motte-and-bailey fortification. Indeed, the first mention of the present castle, in October 1223, speaks of 'the new castle which the king is building outside Montgomery' and a charter of 1229 mentions tenements 'in old and in new Montgomery'.

The Norman hold on Powys, and indeed Ceredigion, was not to last. By the thirteenth century Montgomery was no longer a base behind the Norman advance into Wales but once more a front-line fortification. Throughout the later twelfth and early thirteenth centuries, the Welsh had gradually rebuffed the

The section of Domesday Book *which records that Earl Roger built a castle at Montgomery, the site of which has been identified as Hen Domen, just a short distance from the modern town (The National Archives: PRO, E 31/1/2).*

Careful excavation of the remains of the motte-and-bailey castle at Hen Domen has enabled archaeologists to identify several periods of occupation. This artist's reconstruction shows how the earth-and-timber buildings and defences of the early castle may have looked. (Illustration by Peter Scholefield).

Norman invaders and regained Powys and much of Ceredigion. By 1216 the area around Montgomery was in Welsh hands, controlled not by the fickle prince of southern Powys, Gwenwynwyn (d. 1216), but by Llywelyn ab Iorwerth, prince of Gwynedd, who was to exercise leadership over much of native Wales until his death in 1240.

The move from Hen Domen and the building of the present castle were therefore closely connected with the political and military situation at the beginning of the reign of King Henry III. The death of his father, King John (1199–1216), had left the nine-year-old heir to the throne with an invading French army in possession of much of southern England. Just before his death, however, John had granted the region of Montgomery to Gwenwynwyn in an attempt to secure this vulnerable borderland, but almost immediately it was seized by Llywelyn ab Iorwerth. Llywelyn, married to an illegitimate daughter of King John, was allied with the baronial and French opposition against the king, and when peace with the French was finally restored, the strengthening of the defences of the Welsh March was high on the agenda of the king's ministers. Pre-eminent amongst

these were William Marshal, earl of Pembroke (d. 1219), and Hubert de Burgh, later earl of Kent (d. 1243), both of whom played major roles in defending the realm during the crisis. Moreover, as Marcher lords, they stood to lose land from any further eastward advance by Llywelyn, whose custody of Gwenwynwyn's lands and the frontier district of Montgomery was confirmed in 1218 in the Treaty of Worcester, albeit until Gwenwynwyn's heirs came of age. Similarly, Llywelyn, recognizing the weakness of his southern boundary hereabouts, sought to bolster his support from the rulers of neighbouring districts along the border between Ceri and Brecon and thereby secure the route between Gwynedd and south Wales. Moreover, by detaching these lesser Welsh rulers from their acquiescence to Norman rule with promises of military support, he could strengthen his claim to be prince throughout Wales. It was therefore imperative for the Crown to secure this vulnerable frontier position, and when the royal army successfully regained the Montgomery area from Llywelyn in the autumn of 1223, Henry III chose a new site for his stone castle, leaving Hen Domen to serve as an outpost close to Rhyd Chwima.

Llywelyn ab Iorwerth (d. 1240) was the architect of Gwynedd's supremacy in the early years of the thirteenth century and he held the Montgomery area between about 1216 and 1223. This finely carved stone head, recovered from Llywelyn's castle at Degannwy in north Wales, may represent the prince himself (National Museums & Galleries of Wales).

Henry III and Montgomery Castle

This schematic drawing of Montgomery Castle is probably the earliest known illustration of a Welsh castle and appears in Matthew Paris's Chronica Majora *(The Master and Fellows of Corpus Christi College, Cambridge, Ms. 16, f. 57r [61r]).*

On 30 September 1223, fresh from raising Llywelyn's siege of Builth Castle, the boy king and his army arrived at Montgomery (Hen Domen). It must have been clear that this site could no longer be defended adequately by an obsolete earth-and-timber castle and the decision to build a new stone fortification, rather than update the old, may have been anticipated at least a month earlier. In August carpenters had been put to work near Much Wenlock in Shropshire making brattices (prefabricated wooden palisades) 'to fortify Montgomery Castle when the need arises'. The chronicler, Matthew Paris, recorded that the king's advisers pointed out to him a site 'suitable for the erection of an impregnable castle', and included a marginal drawing of the new *Castrum montis Gomerici* in his manuscript — probably the earliest known illustration of a Welsh castle. Matthew Paris, however, a monk of St Albans, had never set eyes on Montgomery Castle, and the drawing is purely schematic. Behind the bland phrase 'the king's advisers' was the formidable figure of Hubert de Burgh, the king's justiciar (first minister). His battle honours included two prolonged and hard-fought sieges defending the castles at Chinon

in western France in 1204–05 and at Dover in 1216 against the French. He also built and refurbished a number of castles of his own, including those at Skenfrith and Grosmont in the southern March, using the most up-to-date military architecture.

The site chosen for the new castle was on a ridge of metamorphosed limestone, high above the surrounding plain, and, although it was already autumn and the building season was nearly over, work began apace. Twenty miners from the Forest of Dean were set to 'do certain works at the castle', no doubt digging the rock-cut ditches with picks, levers and wedges, and sinking the well through over 200 feet (60m) of rock. Carpenters under the king's master carpenter, Robert de Albemunt, worked alongside them, building a timber castle using the prefabricated brattices, which could be replaced in stone over the coming years. Progress must have been rapid for by November the king was making arrangements for divine service to be performed in the 'new castle of Montgomery'.

Work in stone probably began in the year 1224. Only the inner ward, at the highest point of the ridge, was built in stone at this stage, the middle ward defences remaining in timber until 1251–53. Built on an almost impregnable site, with successive lines of defence and dominated by the inner ward with its twin-towered gatehouse and flanking towers, Montgomery was at the forefront of castle design.

Between 1223 and 1228, more than £3,600 was spent on building work, the wages of the garrison, and the clearance of surrounding woodland to prevent a surprise attack on the fortress. At the same time, the owners of mottes in the Vale of Montgomery were ordered to strengthen them 'for our security and the defence of those parts' indicating that, despite the royal presence, the Welsh remained a conspicuous threat. This fear was indeed well grounded for in August 1228 the castle — which had been granted to Hubert de Burgh in April, with grants of money for its upkeep and a promise of more in case of war — was attacked by Llywelyn ab Iorwerth, anxious to prevent the ambitious justiciar from establishing a foothold in the neighbouring district of Ceri. Although the Welsh prince failed to take the castle, Hubert de Burgh was humiliated and in September peace was concluded. Clearly, the castle was well provisioned for the accounts record '11 tuns of wine from Bruges … for the king's use when he was with his army in the Vale of Kerry'. A year later building work resumed with a grant of £166 13s. 4d. towards the cost of 'enclosing' the castle — which perhaps included the complex of outworks between the outer ditch and the present farm. Llywelyn attacked again in 1231 and although he did not take the castle he seems to have burned down the town newly established below it.

A town seems to have been planned with the castle from the outset (pp. 8–9). By 1224, a new parish had been created out of the large Saxon minster parish of Chirbury and a parson appointed. Traders were encouraged to settle in Montgomery with an offer of the privileges already enjoyed by the burgesses of Shrewsbury, and in 1227 the king's charter to the new borough gave the burgesses the right to hold fairs and markets and to enclose the town with a ditch and wall.

In 1232 Hubert de Burgh fell from power and Montgomery reverted to the Crown. A year later 'the tower' (probably the inner gatehouse) was roofed in lead, and in 1234 the large sum of £86 was spent on repairing the well tower, which may have been suffering structural problems as a result of its unusual construction (pp. 45–46). By this time, however, the inner ward appears to have been essentially complete and later activity was probably in the nature of care and maintenance rather than new works.

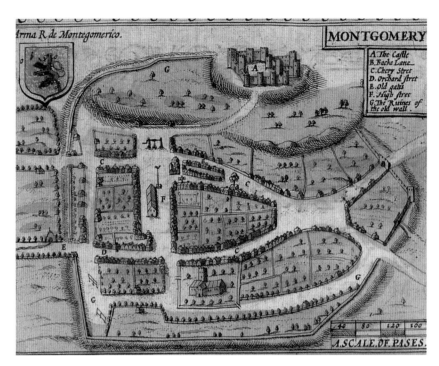

Two surveys, one of 1249 and another of about 1250, provide a helpful insight into the internal arrangements of the castle at this time. Between them, they list the 'donjon' (inner ward) and the 'old hall within the donjon', built of arched timbers or crucks (*furcis*), with a timber bakehouse and kitchen — predecessors of the existing bakehouse and brewhouse (pp. 46–47). There is also mention of a porter's lodge, which was probably located in the inner gatehouse, and a chapel with a 'knight's chamber' nearby. The drawbridge of the inner ward had recently been repaired and there was a 'new hall', probably in the middle ward. Here, the castle was still of timber, and there are references to various brattices (timber palisades), along with stables, a grange, a 'barbican outside the gate' and a road 400 yards (365m) long, cut through the rock between the castle and town. Between 1251 and 1253 the constable, Guy de Rocheford, carried out a major building programme at the castle, including replacing a timber gate with a new twin-towered gatehouse of stone — presumably that in the middle ward. Guy must also have been responsible for replacing the timber defences around the middle ward with the existing stone curtain wall.

Above: A town seems to have been planned from the outset at Montgomery. This plan of 1610, drawn by John Speed, shows both the castle and town defences in a good state of repair.

Hubert de Burgh was granted Montgomery Castle in 1228 but his humiliation by the Welsh and rivalry at court led to his downfall in 1232, when he was deprived of his lands, castles and position as justiciar. He is shown in this mid-thirteenth-century manuscript illustration taking sanctuary at Merton Priory, Surrey (British Library, Royal Ms. 14 C VII, f. 119).

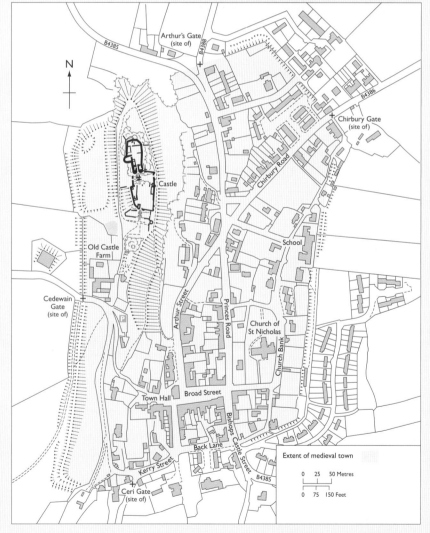

The Town of Montgomery

From the Norman conquest onwards, the new castles founded along the Welsh March were not simply military strongholds. One of their main functions was to make possible the profitable exploitation of the surrounding territory by their lords. For this purpose, a market town was needed, where country people could exchange goods and produce; tolls and taxes could be collected; craftspeople could set up shop; and periodic fairs could be held for the sale of livestock. Towns also played an important role in the process of the Anglo-Norman colonization of Wales.

It was therefore no doubt planned from the outset that a new borough would be established alongside the new castle at Montgomery. As early as November 1223, the king was encouraging traders to supply his castle by offering them safe conduct and the same liberties to trade as those enjoyed by the burgesses of Shrewsbury. Four years later, in 1227, the town received its first charter from the king and, like the earlier inducement, it was based on privileges already held by an older established borough of the March, but this time it was Hereford. The charter speaks of 'those who shall come to live or to trade' and contains a provision that 'the burgesses of the said town may enclose the same with ditch and wall'.

The large market square, around which the eighteenth-century red-brick houses of Montgomery now stand, presided over by the fine town hall of 1748, thus has a long history. The outline of the medieval and later burgage plots can still be traced in the present layout of the town.

The early thirteenth-century church of St Nicholas is the oldest surviving building in Montgomery and dates from when the borough was established. It was necessary to make provision for the burial and spiritual welfare of the town's inhabitants, so a new parish was carved out of the huge Saxon minster parish of Chirbury and the first rector was appointed. The church contains a fifteenth-century wooden screen and stalls, said to be from Chirbury Priory, as well as the magnificent painted and canopied tomb of Richard Herbert

(d.1596) and his wife Magdalene, and the effigy of Sir Edmund Mortimer (d. 1408).

By the 1250s the town was protected by a substantial earthen bank and ditch, crowned with wooden defences. These defences were soon reinforced, at least in part, with a stone wall fronting the bank, sections of which can still be seen around the outskirts of the town (there is a good example on the north, at Arthur's Gate). Access to the town was controlled by four gates and further defence was provided by mural towers at points where the line of the defences changed direction.

Excavations, both at the castle and within the town, show that a flourishing local pottery industry was supplemented by decorated jugs and other vessels brought from a distance by traders. A few vessels, perhaps originally containing drink or luxury foodstuffs, came from France, Spain and the Rhineland, and demonstrate Montgomery's links with the outside world. Certainly, by the thirteenth and fourteenth centuries, Montgomery seems to have been a sizeable and prosperous borough — holding as many as four annual fairs — which did not decline significantly until the advent of the railway and canal in the nineteenth century.

Many of the finds from Hen Domen and Montgomery Castle are displayed at the Old Bell Museum in Arthur Street which also contains a fascinating range of material illustrating all aspects of life in a Welsh border town during the last two centuries.

Llywelyn ap Gruffudd and Dolforwyn Castle

Llywelyn ab Iorwerth had died in 1240 leaving a fragile federation of Welsh princes nominally under the overlordship of his son and heir, Dafydd (d. 1246). But internal dissension and a strong royal hand soon reduced Dafydd's power and it was not until 1258 that another prince of Gwynedd emerged as the undisputed leader of the Welsh — the grandson of Llywelyn ab Iorwerth, Llywelyn ap Gruffudd.

In 1254, however, the royal castle of Montgomery was granted to the Lord Edward — later King Edward I — the son and heir of King Henry III. By now fortified in stone throughout, the castle retained its role as a bastion against Welsh expansion by both the prince of southern Powys, Gruffudd ap Gwenwynwyn (d. 1286), and more especially Llywelyn ap Gruffudd.

Gruffudd ap Gwenwynwyn held Powis Castle, near Welshpool, but, anxious to prevent the Gwynedd prince from gaining control of his lands, he sought to retain his independence through alliances with the Crown and the English barons of the Marches. In contrast, Llywelyn was anxious to assert his role as the most powerful prince in Wales and receive homage from other Welsh-born rulers; in 1257 he invaded the valley of the Severn and occupied the country as far as Welshpool, forcing Gruffudd ap Gwenwynwyn to flee. Montgomery itself was attacked and the town destroyed once more. Just months before, Llywelyn had overrun Roger Mortimer's lordship of Gwrtheyrnion and in 1262 he captured and destroyed Mortimer's castle at Cefnllys, Powys. By 1263 Llywelyn had acquired the disputed districts of Cedewain and Ceri, west of Montgomery, claimed on the one hand by Gruffudd ap Gwenwynwyn as part of Powys and on the other by Roger Mortimer (d.1282). Although Gruffudd ap Gwenwynwyn submitted to Llywelyn and reluctantly agreed to this arrangement in December 1263, this dispute and the threat posed by its proximity to the royal stronghold at Montgomery were to dominate events over the next two decades.

Nevertheless, Llywelyn's territorial gains and his title as prince of Wales were formally recognized by Henry III in return for his fealty and homage under the terms of the Treaty of Montgomery, agreed at the ford of Rhyd Chwima on 19 September 1267.

A manuscript illustration of Llywelyn ab Iorwerth on his deathbed attended by his sons, Gruffudd (d. 1244) and Dafydd (d. 1246), from Matthew Paris's Chronica Majora. *Dafydd, Llywelyn's chosen heir, survived his father by only six years, during which time English royal authority was reasserted in Wales (The Master and Fellows of Corpus Christi College, Cambridge, Ms. 16, f. 133).*

The 1267 Treaty of Montgomery, under the terms of which King Henry III recognized Llywelyn ap Gruffudd's title as prince of Wales and his territorial gains (The National Archives: PRO, E 36/274, f. 327).

Opposite: In 1273 construction of Llywelyn's new castle at Dolforwyn commenced. Its position, on a high ridge overlooking the Severn valley just 4 miles (6.5km) from Montgomery, was a threat to both the king and to the Welsh prince, Gruffudd ap Gwenwynwyn (d. 1286), based at nearby Welshpool. The main features of the Welsh castle are clear in this aerial view and bear a striking resemblance to Dinas Brân, near Llangollen (p. 30), built most probably in the 1260s by Llywelyn's new ally Gruffudd ap Madog (Clwyd–Powys Archaeological Trust).

This was the high water mark of Llywelyn's achievement and gave official recognition to his status as feudal overlord of the majority of independent Welsh rulers. It also showed a need to pacify Llywelyn after the part he had played in the Barons' War led by Simon de Montfort (d. 1265) against Henry III; the prince was betrothed to marry Simon's daughter, Eleanor. However, the treaty led to resentment from both Gruffudd ap Gwenwynwyn and Roger Mortimer, who built afresh at Cefnllys in violation of the 1267 treaty.

In 1270 the Lord Edward left England to go on crusade, leaving his lands in the care of a council of five custodians — three bishops and two barons, one of whom was Roger Mortimer. Two years later, when King Henry III died, the members of this council became regents acting on behalf of the new king. By 1273 Llywelyn's position in Cedewain was vulnerable and in order to protect the district from attack he began to build a castle and town at Dolforwyn, near Abermule, just 4 miles (6.5km) from Montgomery on the opposite side of the Severn. This 'new castle above the Severn' was a challenge not only to the royal frontier post at Montgomery, but also to Gruffudd ap Gwenwynwyn's capital at Welshpool and to the Mortimer interests in Wales. On 23 June 1273 Edward, or more accurately the regents acting in his name, wrote to Llywelyn complaining that he had started 'the repair and construction of the said castle'. In his aggrieved reply less than three weeks later Llywelyn stated that as prince of Wales he did not need royal consent to build a castle on his own land and that the letter must have been sent in the king's name without his knowledge, for Edward was still overseas. Although the wording of Edward's letter ('repair and construction') could be taken to imply that a castle already stood on the site — perhaps the work of Llywelyn ab Iorwerth's son, Dafydd, between 1228 and 1241 — excavation has shown that the Welsh castle was probably all of one period and can be associated with the well-documented work of 1273–77. Indeed, documents show that between April 1273 and April 1274, when Llywelyn himself came on a tour of inspection, the prince's castellan, Bleddyn ap Llywelyn, spent £174 6s. 8d. on the work at the castle.

Dolforwyn, like Montgomery, was erected on a high ridge of shaly rock on the summit of which a platform measuring some 240 feet by 90 feet (72m x 27m) was levelled for the new castle. Work began with a rectangular keep-like tower at the south-west end of the castle and a circular tower at the opposite end. Initially free-standing, they were soon joined by a stone curtain wall to create a rectangular ward, incorporating a D-shaped tower to the north. The courtyard was divided in two by a rock-cut ditch, and a two-storey building was erected against the north curtain. The main entrance was through a simple gateway at the west end of the castle, via the town, with a small subsidiary gate to the south. Dolforwyn is comparable to other castles of the Welsh princes (p. 30), including those of Llywelyn's grandfather, Llywelyn ab Iorwerth, and shows little sign of the more advanced styles of military architecture of the thirteenth century seen, for example, at Caerphilly.

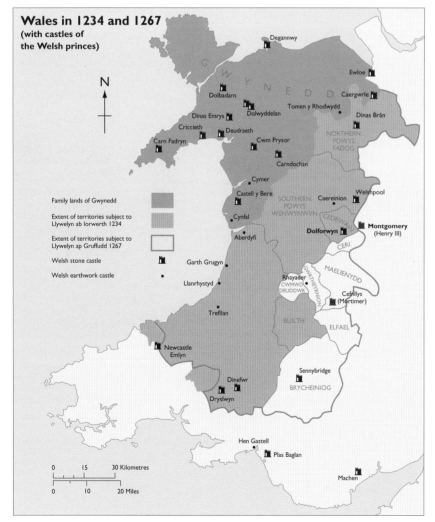

Wales in 1234 and 1267
(with castles of the Welsh princes)

N

Family lands of Gwynedd

Extent of territories subject to Llywelyn ab Iorwerth 1234

Extent of territories subject to Llywelyn ap Gruffudd 1267

Welsh stone castle

Welsh earthwork castle

The new castle was soon put to the test when, in 1274, Llywelyn learned about a plot against his life. This was led by his duplicitous brother, Dafydd (d. 1283), who was lured by the prospect of becoming prince of Wales, and Gruffudd ap Gwenwynwyn — who hoped to recover Ceri and Cedewain. Gruffudd was summoned to meet his overlord at Dolforwyn and there required to give up his son, Owain, as a hostage for his loyalty and good behaviour. However, it seems that the enormity of the plot was not revealed in its entirety until later the

This imaginative illustration of King Edward I (1272–1307) attended by Llywelyn, prince of Wales, appears in a sixteenth-century manuscript. It was the failure of Llywelyn to pay homage to the king as required that provoked Edward's invasion of Wales in 1277 (The Royal Library, Wriothesley Ms. quire B; The Royal Collection © 2004, Her Majesty Queen Elizabeth II).

Large siege engines, such as that seen in this manuscript illustration, were employed at Dolforwyn in the spring of 1277, and on 8 April the Welsh garrison surrendered the damaged castle (British Library, Additional Ms. 10294, f. 81v).

same year. Gruffudd was summoned once more to answer the accusation but rather than face the wrath of Llywelyn he fled to Shrewsbury to live under English royal protection, as did his co-conspirator, Dafydd. Llywelyn responded in characteristic fashion: *Brut y Tywysogyon* records that he 'overran all of the territory of Gruffudd without opposition and set his own officers over it all'. Unwilling to pay homage to a king that sheltered his enemies and who in 1275–76 had captured Eleanor de Montfort, his wife-to-be, Llywelyn refused to leave Wales without a trustworthy safe-conduct. No such assurance was forthcoming and despite numerous royal summonses, Llywelyn persistently failed to attend on Edward I, though he sought to defend his actions in correspondence with the king.

Edward was not to be pacified and during the autumn of 1276 he prepared for war with Llywelyn. In the spring of 1277 hostilities broke out between England and Wales with the king launching a three-pronged attack on the principality from Chester, Carmarthen and Montgomery. On 31 March, Dolforwyn was closely besieged by Roger Mortimer with support from the royal cavalry led by Henry de Lacy, earl of Lincoln (d. 1311). Large siege engines were brought to the site, the sheriff of Hereford claiming 24s. for the transport of a catapult from Wigmore to Dolforwyn. That the siege engines were used to good effect is demonstrated by the damaged corners of the square keep revealed during excavation (p. 27).

Water soon ran short (the castle, unlike Montgomery, then had no well) and the garrison was forced to negotiate with the besiegers. They agreed to surrender if Llywelyn did not relieve the castle by 8 April. Such agreements were not uncommon in castle sieges and, when no help arrived by the stipulated date, the garrison surrendered. The earl of Lincoln reported to the king that the castle had suffered much damage and would need repair. The prince of Powys, Gruffudd ap Gwenwynwyn, was given custody of the castle briefly, but in the following year it was granted to Roger Mortimer, along with the lands of Ceri and Cedewain.

The fall of Dolforwyn was part of Edward I's pincer movement around Llywelyn's lands in Gwynedd. He sought to consolidate his victory with the construction of new castles in north-east Wales at Flint and Rhuddlan, in mid-Wales at Builth and also

at Aberystwyth in Ceredigion, where Llywelyn might have expected to gain support from Welsh lords south of the river Dyfi. The military campaign was underpinned by an economic takeover with each new castle being supported by a new town. In 1279 Roger Mortimer replaced Llywelyn's incipient borough outside the walls of Dolforwyn with a settlement a short distance away in the Severn valley, which is still known as Newtown.

The corners of the square keep, damaged in the siege, were repaired by Master Bertram the Engineer, but the repair of Dolforwyn was also accompanied by the improvement of Montgomery's defences. Between 1278 and 1280, under the constableship of Bogo de Knovil, the wooden palisades on the bank and ditch around the town

of Montgomery were taken down and replaced by a stone wall — at least in part — sections of which can still be seen. These improvements were clearly appropriate for a castle as significant as Montgomery, which for much of the time until the construction of Edward's new castles, was the only major royal base in north and central Wales. It had been crucial in 1277 as one of the key bases from which royal expeditions were launched against Llywelyn and it was here, in 1278, that the Hopton commission met on no less than twenty-one occasions (out of a total of thirty-eight) to review the legal situation in Wales. Small wonder then that contemporaries writing in the fourteenth-century claimed that 'the greater part of Wales was conquered from the lordship of Montgomery'.

An artist's impression showing the siege of Dolforwyn and the destruction of Llywelyn's small town in front of the main entrance to the castle. Although the keep, round tower and apsidal tower were probably complete by this time, the north range is the only wholly domestic building known to have been erected in the courtyard (Illustration by Ivan Lapper 2002).

Right: This manuscript illustration depicts the death of Llywelyn ap Gruffudd, the first and last Welsh prince of Wales, which took place at a skirmish near Builth Wells in December 1282 (British Library, Cotton Nero Ms. D II, f. 182).

Below: By about 1280 both the castle and parts of the town of Montgomery were defended with stone walls. This artist's impression of the castle at this time suggests that the north-western section of the town wall was masonry-built and that there may have been an additional gate here. The outworks are shown defended with wooden palisades (Illustration by Ivan Lapper 2002).

Despite the humiliating defeat suffered by Llywelyn in 1277, he was forced into the field once more, albeit perhaps reluctantly, when his brother, Dafydd, rebelled in 1282 against English domination. The last native prince of Wales was killed in a skirmish at Cilmeri outside Builth Wells on 11 December 1282 and less than a year later his brother was captured and executed at Shrewsbury. In response to this victory, and to ensure the submission of the Welsh, Edward I began to build yet more castles — at Harlech, Caernarfon and Conwy — to control the newly conquered territory of Gwynedd (p. 44). Consequently, Montgomery ceased to be a front-line castle of military importance and, although a new hall, chamber, kitchen, bakehouse and granary were built between 1283 and 1288, there was no new work on the defences. Nevertheless, in 1294–95 Montgomery was once more one of three

key bases from which a royal military campaign was waged against a widespread Welsh revolt.

During the first half of the fourteenth century, Montgomery seems to have been in a sad state of neglect. In 1310 a newly appointed constable, Hugh Audele, gave a melancholy 'list of defects which are in the castle of Montgomery'. The lead on the gatehouse roof was faulty and the 'chief tower' (presumably the well tower) about to fall down. What few armaments there were in the castle — shields, helmets and the like — were old and perished and apart from 'a pot of brass, old and broken' there were no kitchen vessels. The scarcity of Edwardian coins from Montgomery contrasts with the discovery of ten Edwardian coins at Dolforwyn, which suggests that occupation at the latter was more intense. Moreover, excavation at Dolforwyn has revealed various modifications to the Welsh-built castle including alterations to the square keep, where a new door was inserted and the main room partitioned. The south gate was blocked up, new domestic buildings were constructed on both sides of the courtyard and a well was dug, no doubt to avoid a repetition of the events of the 1277 siege.

The Earls of March

Montgomery continued to be a royal castle, and therefore the gift of the king to bestow on those who would best serve his interests in the area. Consequently, Montgomery was often in the hands of the Mortimers — the most powerful family of the local nobility; Dolforwyn, however, became a baronial castle. It was also granted to the Mortimers, but in perpetuity, except when they forfeited the castle through treason. Thus, a relatively well-documented history of Montgomery survives in royal accounts, since it was the king's duty to pay for its repair, whereas records of Dolforwyn are limited to periods when the castle was taken into royal hands, or when its owner died.

After the death of Roger Mortimer in 1282, his territories passed to his son, Edmund, who held them until his death in 1304. Edmund's son and heir, Roger (d. 1330), lost the family lands in 1322, when he was imprisoned for treason, but a year later he escaped and fled to France where he met Isabella (d.1358), the estranged wife of King Edward II (1307–27).

He returned from exile in 1326, by now the queen's companion as well as her political ally, and in 1328 was created the first earl of March. In April 1330 Montgomery and Dolforwyn were returned to Earl Roger, but both castles and lands reverted to the Crown in November the same year when, amongst a long list of felonies, he was found guilty and executed for his part in Edward II's murder at Berkeley Castle.

Little is known about Montgomery during Earl Roger's tenure of the castle; however, somewhat unexpectedly, an inventory of Dolforwyn, made by a royal clerk, survives from January 1322 when the castle was confiscated. This records the buildings, many of which have been confirmed by excavation and are visible today. There are references to the round tower, which housed the castle armoury, the square tower, a hall and chapel, and a lady's chamber (complete with a tub for bathing). The inventory also lists various service rooms — pantry, buttery (for the service of drinks), kitchen, brewhouse, bakehouse, two garners for the storage of grain and a grange (home farm) outside the castle.

The archaeological evidence revealed by the excavation of the castle complements this picture of life at Dolforwyn in the early fourteenth century. The hall was fitted out with a hearth, paved floor and plastered walls; the latter embellished with coloured paintings. Fragments from stained glass windows, a decorated floor tile and an ivory book cover with the

Made in January 1322, when Dolforwyn was confiscated from Roger Mortimer (d. 1330), this inventory of the castle provides a remarkable insight into the buildings and their contents (The National Archives: PRO, E 101/15/39).

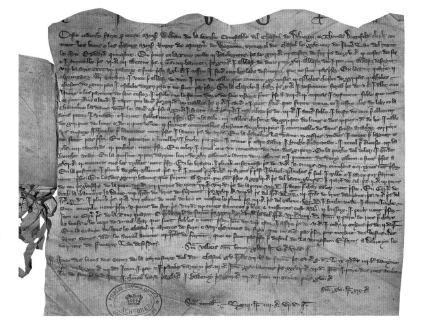

An artist's impression of Dolforwyn Castle in about 1320. In contrast to the Welsh castle (p. 13), the courtyard now contains numerous service and domestic buildings, including a bakehouse and brewhouse, a hall and a well. The south gate has been blocked up and little remains of the town since Roger Mortimer (d. 1282) established a new borough in the valley bottom at what is still known as Newtown (Illustration by Ivan Lapper 2002).

figure of a saint, confirm the presence of a chapel, though its exact location remains uncertain. There were glazed pots, a bowl from Merida in southern Spain, and glass vessels from the kitchen; the bakehouse contained evidence of three well-constructed ovens and in the brewhouse there was the base of two vats, a roasting hearth and a steeping trough. Elsewhere smithy furnaces, horseshoes and mortar-mixing floors reflect industrial activity at the castle. In contrast, beads of shale and amber, hat badges, a large number of dice and jettons (coin-like counters used in casting accounts), an ivory ball and tuning pegs for a stringed musical instrument — probably a Welsh *crwth* or bowed lyre (p. 38) — hint at a comfortable domestic life.

Earl Roger's son, Edmund, inherited Dolforwyn and Montgomery in 1330, but when he died two

years later, his son, Roger (d. 1360), was still a minor so the lands and castles returned once more to royal hands. In 1343 they were granted to Edward, the Black Prince (d. 1376) and only returned to Roger — who had been created second earl of March in 1354 — following the reversal of his grandfather's attainder in 1359.

In 1331, however, repairs costing £20 were made to the drawbridge and to the castle buildings at Montgomery. The townspeople were given a murage grant, or tax relief, for four years, to permit a programme of repair work on the town walls between 1336 and 1340. Despite this expenditure, when the castle was granted to Edward the Black Prince in 1343 his commissioners reported that the Black and White Towers (the gatehouse and well tower) were falling into ruin and that the curtain walls of both baileys were weak. The king provided timber for the work at the castle, and for the work on the town walls.

In 1359, Montgomery and Dolforwyn were returned to the Mortimers and although the family held a number of other Marcher castles, including their principal seat at Wigmore, Montgomery appears to have been maintained to a high standard. Several finds confirm the high status of the accommodation, including a painted glass panel, finely decorated with the head of a lady wearing a headband or diadem. Other fragments of glass painted with lion masks and sherds of a jar of archaic Italian maiolica ware, a rare import at this date, all point to a residence of some luxury.

The middle ward contained service buildings at this time, including a kiln house in which grain could be dried or roasted. Whether the kiln was designed to roast grain for the making of malt, or whether the wetter climate of late medieval Britain made the drying of grain before storage necessary, is uncertain. Next to the kiln house were lightly constructed timber-framed buildings, built on stone foundations, which may have been used by estate workers. Just as at Dolforwyn, finds included jettons and tuning pegs from a musical instrument, probably a Welsh *crwth* (p. 38). Montgomery was not only still a high status residence, but also the centre of an active agricultural estate.

Although Dolforwyn remained in some sort of use, for coins continued to be 'lost' there until the reign of Richard II (1377–99), the castle does not seem to have been kept in a good state of repair. In 1381 it was described as in 'a poor state of repair and worth nothing', and in 1398 it was 'ruinous and worth nothing' suggesting that the lead roofs and the window glass had all been removed. Despite the Owain Glyn Dŵr rebellion in the opening years of the fifteenth century, it appears that Dolforwyn was no longer of use to the king and was not repaired by the Mortimers. Montgomery, in contrast, was garrisoned for the king in 1402–03 with 60 men-at-arms and 124 archers, and a substantial force seems to have been retained until 1407–08, suggesting that the castle was essential to the English strategy to contain the revolt. However, once the revolt had subsided the castle received little save routine maintenance.

Despite the disgrace of Roger, first earl of March, the Mortimer family soon regained royal favour. In 1348 Roger's grandson — another Roger — became a founder member of the Order of the Garter and in 1354 he was created second earl of March. This fifteenth-century manuscript illustration of Earl Roger is from the Bruges Garter Book *(British Library, Stowe Ms. 594, f. 15v).*

Painted Glass

Among the evidence that Montgomery was still a place of importance and status under the earls of March is a panel of painted glass found in a layer of sixteenth-century rubble fill during excavation. It shows a lady with flowing hair, wearing a flowered headband, or diadem, and a low-cut gown. Datable, on stylistic grounds, to around 1350, it is thought to belong to a school of glass painting in the Welsh borders characteristic of the mid-fourteenth century. Other examples, from churches at Madeley (Herefordshire), Ludlow (Shropshire) and Hadzor (Worcestershire), are saints and prophets, including a very similar head of the Virgin Mary from Hadzor. However, the Montgomery panel shows a secular lady of high rank. Its scale suggests that it was meant to be seen not high up in a church window, but at close range, perhaps in the castle chapel.

A panel of mid-fourteenth-century painted glass depicting a lady of high rank, found at Montgomery Castle (The Old Bell Museum, Montgomery).

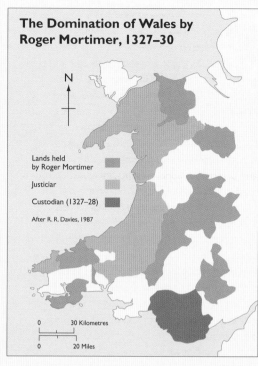

The Domination of Wales by Roger Mortimer, 1327–30

N

Lands held by Roger Mortimer

Justiciar

Custodian (1327–28)

After R. R. Davies, 1987

0   30 Kilometres

0   20 Miles

Above: Roger Mortimer IV (d. 1330) is shown in this late fifteenth-century manuscript illustration meeting Queen Isabella (d. 1358), the estranged wife of King Edward II (1307–27), with whom he plotted to capture and depose the king (British Library, Royal Ms. 15 E IV, f. 316v).

Below: Part of the gatehouse at Wigmore Castle, Herefordshire, the principal seat of the Mortimer family until the fourteenth century (English Heritage).

The Mortimers — Lords of the March

Roger of Mortemer originated from Mortemer, north of Rouen, in upper Normandy and, like many of the burgeoning aristocracy gathered around Duke William, he supported the Conqueror's expedition to England in 1066. Wales, however, lay beyond the direct interest of the new king, and in order to protect the border he created three earldoms under the control of his most trusted commanders: William fitz Osbern, earl of Hereford (d. 1071); Roger of Montgomery, earl of Shrewsbury (d. 1094); and Hugh of Avranches, earl of Chester (d. 1101). Each was granted royal estates and the earls ruled with a remarkable degree of independence, granting land and privileges to their own loyal supporters. This was the foundation of the March itself, which came to represent a fluctuating group of lordships acquired piecemeal through private colonization bordering that part of Wales ruled by the Welsh princes — *pura Wallia*.

Roger's son, Ralph, appears to have been held in high esteem by both William fitz Osbern and Roger of Montgomery, whom he served as steward, and held lands at Wigmore in Herefordshire —

including the castle, which became the family's principal seat until the fourteenth century — as well as in eleven other counties. By 1100 he had conquered Maelienydd (later in Radnorshire), probably as part of Earl Roger's campaigns into mid-Wales (p. 4), and built the castle of Cymaron on the site of the former Welsh court, or *llys*.

Support for the Crown throughout the twelfth century ensured that the Mortimers enjoyed a special relationship as tenants-in-chief to the king for their west-Midland estate, receiving privileges and exemptions that were to promote and safeguard the family interests. Judicious marriages with the daughter of Llywelyn ab Iorwerth and the de Braose family secured new lands and also proved useful in negotiations with both the Welsh and other Marcher lords. Nor did they neglect their spiritual needs, founding an abbey at Wigmore in the late twelfth century, which served as a family mausoleum for the following three centuries.

Such was the strength of the foundations of the Mortimer family when Roger III, lord of Wigmore

(d. 1282), rose to a position of national importance. He was high in the king's favour, held many castles, administered royal estates and sat on the royal council. He served King Henry III in England, Wales and Ireland; supported Prince Edward, the future king, in battles against the rebellious Simon de Montfort; and later fought against his cousin Llywelyn ap Gruffudd. His military prowess was a decisive factor in bringing him lucrative and prestigious appointments, including the lordships of Ceri and Cedewain, with Dolforwyn Castle (pp. 12–13), near which he established the successful borough of Newtown — and thereby secured another source of income. It is not therefore surprising that Roger is credited as 'one of the great architects of the late medieval March'.

Roger IV, who had succeeded to the Mortimer estates on the death of his father Edmund (d. 1304) was a key figure in the March of Wales and in Ireland in the early fourteenth century. But in 1322 he fell foul of Edward II and his favourite, the young Despenser, and was imprisoned in the Tower. He escaped to France and there became friendly with Edward's queen, Isabella, and together they led the force that captured, deposed and eventually arranged the death of the king. During the years 1327–30 Mortimer was virtually the governor of England under the young Edward III. He assembled a huge empire for himself, especially in Wales and Ireland, and secured the new title of earl of March in 1328, a recognition of where his power base lay. But in 1330 Edward and his supporters plotted Mortimer's downfall, secured his execution and confiscated his estates.

The Mortimers, however, staged a recovery in the 1350s and resecured control of Montgomery and Dolforwyn and their associated lordships. Three earls — Roger V (d. 1360), Edmund (d. 1381) and Roger VI (d. 1398) — all died young, and in 1425 the direct male line failed with the death of Earl Edmund. The Mortimer estates — including the lordship of Montgomery — passed through marriage to the house of York, which successfully laid claim to the throne in the person of Edward IV in 1461.

The Mortimers continued to hold the two castles intermittently until 1425 when they reverted to the Crown and thence to Richard, duke of York (d. 1460), who also succeeded to the Mortimer baronies. Following York's forfeiture in 1459, the castles and lands returned to the Crown, and so to Duke Richard's son when he succeeded to the throne as Edward IV in 1461 (1461–70; 1471–83).

The Herbert Family

The sixteenth century saw the beginning of the connection of the Herbert family with Montgomery that has continued to the present day. In 1490 the castle had been granted to Arthur, prince of Wales (d. 1502), and the first mention of a new constable appears in 1504 when Sir Charles Somerset, Lord Herbert (d. 1526), was appointed. In 1492 Sir Charles had married Elizabeth, the heir of William Herbert (of Raglan), earl of Huntingdon (d. 1491), and in consequence was created Lord Herbert; it was his kinsman, Richard Herbert, who seems to have been the first of the family to reside at the castle. Richard Herbert was appointed as the king's receiver in about 1508 and was certainly holding a prisoner at Montgomery in March 1535. He died in 1539 and was buried in Montgomery church, where what is claimed to be his effigy survives.

Sir Richard Herbert (d. 1539) seems to have been the first of the Herbert family to reside at Montgomery Castle. What is claimed to be his tomb effigy now lies in the town church (The Rector and Churchwardens of The Church of St Nicholas, Montgomery).

The magnificent canopied tomb of Sir Richard Herbert (d. 1596) and his wife Magdalene (d. 1627) in the church of St Nicholas, Montgomery. Lady Herbert, in particular, is remembered for her association with the poet John Donne, who may have stayed at the castle (The Rector and Churchwardens of The Church of St Nicholas, Montgomery).

Right: Edward Herbert (d. 1648) led a long and distinguished life as a writer, scholar and diplomat, retiring to his new house built in the middle ward of the castle at Montgomery in about 1624. In 1631, two years after he had been created first Baron Herbert of Chirbury, Sir Edward commissioned the French sculptor, Hubert le Sueur, to make this magnificent bronze bust (National Trust Photographic Library: Andreas von Einsiedel).

In 1534, however, Rowland Lee, bishop of Coventry and Lichfield, had been made Lord President of the Council of Wales and the Marches by Henry VIII (1509–47), a post that he held until his death in 1543. In his capacity as lord president, Lee sought to maintain control over the remaining Marcher lordships not yet in royal possession and to impose law and order on this part of Wales and the March, which had been notoriously disorderly. To this end he set about refortifying the principal royal castles in the Marches and, with characteristic vigour, he began to renovate Montgomery.

The castle had seen little save routine repairs since the time of Edward I and by 1537 Lee was talking of his intended 're-edification of Montgomery Castle, the second key of Wales', requesting that fines levied on rioters in Denbighshire should be spent on works at the castle. By June 1538 there were 100 men at work on the castle and later in the year he spoke of 'Montgomery, where there is no small charge'.

Two years earlier, in 1536, the Augustinian priory at Chirbury had been suppressed and John Leland, writing in 1536–39, noted 'Chirbiri, a priori of Chanons … much of the stone and lead brought to repayre Montgomery' and 'the castell, now a-late re-edified', with a deer park around it.

Excavation has indeed confirmed that much of the building material from Chirbury was brought to Montgomery for work at the castle. The eastern side of the middle ward — between the curtain walls and the central rock ridge — was in-filled with building rubble to create a level platform and excavation has recovered many broken architectural fragments, pieces of medieval floor tile and even scraps of painted glass, which originated from Chirbury. Once the middle ward was level, Lee built a series of lodgings for the numerous officials of his household; he also raised additional accommodation in the inner ward.

The Herbert family continued to rent the castle from the Crown following Lee's death. From 1547 it was held by Sir Richard Herbert's son, Edward (d. 1592), who seems to have preferred to reside at Blackhall — a house that he built in or near the town, though the exact location remains unknown. Clearly, by the time of Sir Edward's death, the accommodation at the castle had deteriorated for a survey of 1592–93 records a poor state of repair and ends with the words 'there ys noe howsholde stuffe in the castell….'

Edward was succeeded by his son, Richard, who survived him by just four years and died in 1596. His magnificent canopied tomb, with fine effigies of himself and his wife, Magdalene (d. 1627), a friend and patron of the poet John Donne (d. 1631), survives in Montgomery church. A poem attributed to Donne, *The Primrose, being at Montgomery Castle upon the Hill, on which it is Situate*, suggests that he may have stayed at the castle, and his closeness to the family is further attested by *The Autumnall*, the subject of which is Lady Herbert herself. Donne also preached her funeral sermon, though by this time Lady Herbert had remarried and consequently was laid to rest in Chelsea, rather than alongside her first husband at Montgomery.

The family inheritance passed to Richard's eldest son, Edward Herbert (d. 1648) — writer, scholar, diplomat and later Lord Herbert of Chirbury. He resided at Montgomery from about 1603 and in 1613 purchased the castle for £500 from his kinsman Philip Herbert, earl of Montgomery and later earl of Pembroke, to whom it had been unaccountably granted in 1607. Later, between 1622 and 1625, Edward Herbert built a fine new house within the middle ward of the castle, which became his home following his retirement as ambassador to Paris in 1624. The house, unfortunately, had a short life, for it was demolished

at the end of the Civil War and virtually nothing now remains. It was built by a family of bricklayers and carpenters named Scampion from Great Hormead on the Essex–Hertfordshire border. Brick was then a novelty in the area, for it was still a building material for the wealthy and those with metropolitan connections. Special kilns had to be built to make the 600,000 bricks needed, plus the cornices and other shaped bricks, which had decorative mouldings cut on their edges.

The entrance to the middle ward was still through the medieval gatehouse, with the main building — a rectangular block — in the south-east corner and a long narrow range behind the west curtain thus creating an L-shaped plan. We know just enough about the building to realize what a grievous loss its destruction was. One room had an elaborate decorated plaster ceiling, the work of 'one Faulkener', many fragments of which were found in excavation. There was also a fine library, for Lord Herbert had an important collection of books. When the castle was surrendered in 1644, one of the conditions was that the soldiers should not go into the library or the room next to it.

The Civil War and Later

In 1642, shortly before the outbreak of the Civil War between King Charles I (1625–49) and parliament, Lord Herbert, by now old, partially deaf and with failing eyesight, retired to his new house at Montgomery. He was disillusioned with the king's policies and refused to take part in the war and, although Montgomery was nominally held for the king, Herbert would not allow Prince Rupert (d. 1682) to install a royalist garrison, instead preferring to rely on a small personal retinue. It was unusual for an elderly civilian to be left in charge of a strategic castle such as Montgomery — most were placed under military governors. Deference to Lord Herbert's distinguished career, his age and influential family may have taken precedence over purely military considerations, particularly in an area which did not seem to be immediately threatened.

For much of the war, Montgomery lay outside the area of active warfare and, like most of Wales, supported the royalist cause. However, shortly after the parliamentarian victory at Marston Moor outside

York in June 1644, which resulted in a collapse of royalist power in northern England, the parliamentarian commander in north Wales, Sir Thomas Myddleton (d. 1666), was ordered to march into Montgomeryshire. He was to secure the area — the gateway to the upper Severn valley and mid-Wales — and disrupt the royalist supply route.

Newtown was raided early in September and, following the successful capture of a royalist powder convoy, the parliamentarians turned their attention to Montgomery. On 4 September, Myddleton appeared

Top: An artist's reconstruction of Sir Edward Herbert's house in the middle ward of Montgomery Castle, built between 1622 and 1625. Sadly, nothing now remains of the house, which was systematically destroyed after the Civil War (1642–48), on account of the royalist sympathies of Lord Herbert's son, Colonel Richard Herbert (d. 1655). The house is known to have contained an important collection of books, the safe removal of which to Lord Herbert's London house was a condition of his surrender in 1644 (Illustration by Neil Ludlow 1993).

Left: The staircase at Lymore Hall, Montgomery, which may have been salvaged from Edward Herbert's house in the middle ward of the castle. The staircase was subsequently removed to Aldborough Hall, near Boroughbridge, Yorkshire.

Above: A mid-seventeenth-century portrait of Sir Thomas Myddleton (d. 1666), the parliamentarian commander of north Wales, who laid siege to Montgomery Castle in September 1644 (National Trust).

Right: Considerable amounts of obsolete armour were recovered from the inner ditch at Montgomery, which may have been abandoned there following the battle in 1644 (p. 41). This reconstruction shows two pikemen dressed in some of the armour (Illustration by Geraint Derbyshire 1991).

William Dobson's portrait of John, first Lord Byron (d. 1652), who commanded the royalist forces in the battle of Montgomery (Tabley House Collection: Bridgeman Art Library).

secretly before Montgomery Castle and, with 200 horse and 500 foot, seized the outer barbican. Lord Herbert's son, the royalist colonel, Richard Herbert (d. 1655), wrote to Prince Rupert that his father hoped to hold out until help came, but the castle was 'ill provided'. By then, however, Lord Herbert, who had only 30 men in the castle, some of whom fled over the walls when the parliamentarian soldiers appeared, had already entered into negotiations with Myddleton. The parliamentarians offered assorted inducements to surrender, including money and promises that Herbert's possessions (especially his books) would be undamaged and conveyed safely to his London house if he so wished. Overnight, Myddleton's master gunner, John Arundell, planted a petard (mine) below the outer gatehouse of the castle and the next day Herbert surrendered. By 6 September Montgomery was garrisoned for parliament.

In quick response, the royalist commander, Sir Michael Ernely, collected troops from the garrisons of Shrewsbury, Ludlow and elsewhere, and laid siege to the castle. Myddleton withdrew to Oswestry whilst his co-commander, Thomas Mytton (d. 1656), held the castle. Ernely was soon joined by Lord Byron (d. 1652), with royalist reinforcements from Chester, including several Anglo-Irish regiments. Byron now assumed command of the combined force, which numbered between 4,000 and 5,000 men, and held the castle under close siege. On 17 September a parliamentary relief force of about 3,000 troops, led by Myddleton, Sir William Fairfax, Sir William Brereton and Sir John Meldrum, who was in overall command, approached Montgomery to relieve the castle. Byron withdrew from his siegeworks and occupied a hill above the town. From here, on 18 September, he attempted to surround the parliamentarian relief troops by seizing a bridge across the river Camlad behind them, and so began the battle of Montgomery.

Many aspects of the battle remain unclear. However, the royalist foot held their ground, and appeared to be at an advantage, when it seems that the Lancashire horse broke and fled (as they had done at Marston Moor), leaving the infantry to their fate. Five hundred royalists were killed and between 1,200 and 1,500 taken prisoner. 'Not a hundred foot came off' confessed a royalist commander, Arthur Trevor. Thus, the last royalist field army in the west was destroyed, and it is possible that the large quantities of somewhat obsolete armour found in the castle

ditch belonged to Byron's Anglo-Irish reinforcements and were dumped soon after their defeat.

Lord Herbert withdrew to his London house after the fall of Montgomery. For a short time, between May and June 1645, when the king appeared to be winning, the castle was recovered for the royalist cause when its governor, Sir John Price, changed sides. The king wrote to him praising his loyalty, but this did not prevent Price — a weathercock who changed sides several times during the war — from reverting to his parliamentary allegiance after the crushing royalist defeat at Naseby.

Lord Herbert died in August 1648 and in that same summer royalist plotters seized the castles at Chepstow and Pembroke and declared for the king. Parliament, fearing similar action from Lord Herbert's heir, Colonel Richard Herbert, wrote to the governor of Shrewsbury that 'the old Lord of Chirbury being dead, and of what affection his son is … you very well know' and ordered that 'the new Lord Chirbury is not to enter the castle'.

In April 1649, Lord Herbert agreed to the slighting of the castle. The outworks were to be destroyed, the ditches filled in, and the 'old' medieval castle demolished. When no local people could be found to carry out the work, Lord Herbert agreed to finance it himself, the costs being deducted from his fine for 'delinquency'. In the event both the old castle and the new house were demolished. Between June and October 1649, up to 150 labourers, as well as miners and skilled craftsmen, were at work demolishing the castle and house, carefully salvaging timber, tiles and glass for future use and profit. In the words of Izaak Walton, 'the heirs of the castle saw it level with that earth, that was too good to bury those wretches that were the cause of it'.

The commissioners who supervised the demolition gave orders 'for the drawing of the old castle, before demolishing the walls', but if any drawing or plan was made, it does not survive. Apart from the schematic view in John Speed's map of 1610, no picture of the castle is known earlier than Samuel and Nathaniel Buck's engraving of 1742, when much more of the castle survived than is visible today. There were serious falls of masonry early in the nineteenth century and what was left stood more or less unchanged until 1963, when the fifth earl of Powis placed the castle in State guardianship. The excavation and consolidation of the ruins began in 1964 and continued until 1981.

Similarly, records of Dolforwyn are sparse and it seems that the castle did not attract much eighteenth-century antiquarian or tourist interest, though a 1776 picture by Moses Griffith (d. 1819) does survive. In 1955, Dr J. D. K. Lloyd, an authority on the history and antiquities of Montgomery, and chairman of the Ancient Monuments Board for Wales, placed Dolforwyn in State care; his grandfather had bought the castle from a previous earl of Powis. A programme of excavation and consolidation began there in 1981 and was completed in 2002. Both castles are now cared for by Cadw on behalf of the National Assembly for Wales.

Below: The ruins of Montgomery Castle in 1742, by Samuel and Nathaniel Buck (National Library of Wales).

Bottom: A 1776 watercolour by Moses Griffith (d. 1819) showing Dolforwyn Castle from the north (National Library of Wales).

A Tour of Dolforwyn Castle

Dolforwyn Castle commands a superb hilltop position overlooking the Severn valley, not far from Abermule, just off the busy A483. The little lanes that lead to a small car park belie the magnificent setting and the impressive remains that await the visitor, and you will be well rewarded for the stiff uphill climb of about 550 yards (500m) from the road.

From the car park take the rough track on the opposite side of the road. The surface is initially of concrete sleeper blocks from the Abermule-Kerry light railway. The track climbs gradually past Yew Tree Cottage on the right and through a wooden gate. Where the track turns sharply right to climb onto the spine of the hill the visitor passes through the site of the small town, founded by Llywelyn ap Gruffudd (p. 10) to serve and protect the castle. Here, you can see several level platforms where half-timbered and thatched houses once stood, probably enclosed by a timber palisade. The town was abandoned after 1277, when the English took control, and a farm, or grange, was established; this, too, would have helped to supply the garrison with food and other resources, together with those garnered from the surrounding region — the commotes of Ceri and Cedewain.

The medieval approach to the castle led through the town, across a timber bridge over a rock-cut ditch to the main gateway. Visitors today, however, should follow the modern track to approach the castle from the northern end of the ditch. Originally, the ditch was much deeper and it was closed at either end by link walls to prevent attackers from setting fire to the timber bridge. The foundations of the north link wall can be seen on your right as you turn into the ditch.

From here, you can either follow the tour route suggested below, or explore the castle for yourself using the ground plan (inside back cover) and bird's-eye view (inside front cover).

The Castle Entrance

Standing outside the entrance to the castle, you can see that the west wall has been badly eroded and only parts of the inner core now remain. Portions of the outer wall face had slid down into the ditch as the rock beneath the wall crumbled from erosion or tree root damage. Fortunately, other parts of the castle fared better and it is clear from excavation and site clearance that the Welsh fortress consisted first

Opposite: Until 1980, very little masonry was thought to survive at Dolforwyn. Some twenty years of excavation later, followed by careful consolidation and presentation work, and the full extent of Llywelyn ap Gruffudd's castle has been revealed together with the modifications made some time after the castle was captured by the English in 1277. This view across the courtyard shows the English-built hall in the foreground with the north range in the background, which was begun by the Welsh prince and subsequently enlarged after 1277.

Above left: The medieval approach to the castle was through the small town that lay on the grassy spur to the west, where several house platforms can still be identified.

Left: The castle was protected by a rock-cut ditch, the ends of which were closed by link walls to prevent attackers from gaining access and setting fire to the timber bridge that spanned the ditch. Only part of the north link wall is visible.

Entrance

Entrance

Below: The English-built guardroom overlooking the much-ruined entrance passage to the castle.

Below right: The ground-floor entrance to the keep was created during the English occupation of the castle. The stairs to the left of the entrance were also modified and made steeper to allow access to the ground-floor doorway. The line of the original Welsh stairs, which gave access to the keep via a door at first-floor level, can also be identified.

of two towers, which were soon linked by a curtain wall incorporating a D-shaped tower to create a rectangular courtyard. Apart from repairs to the existing buildings, the remaining structures, which include most of the courtyard ranges built against the curtain walls, were constructed after the English occupied the castle in 1277.

The modern track crosses the line of the curtain wall to the left of the original gateway, now marked by low walling of thin dark grey-brown slabs, which are characteristic of Welsh-built features. The gateway appears to have been a simple arched opening protected by a strong door, perhaps with a wooden fighting platform above.

Ahead is the keep, and to the right are two rooms built in the south-west angle of the curtain wall. Both rooms are of English construction using large, square grey-brown blocks; that to the right was a guardroom equipped with a window opening on to the Welsh-period entrance passage, a fireplace platform incorporating a millstone and, in the thickness of the south wall, a passage to a double latrine. The adjoining room, built against the keep, was a storeroom with a window at high level, which contains traces of its original lime mortar rendering, and a drawbar hole so that the door could be firmly secured. Outside there seems to have been either a lean-to shed or porch, perhaps connected to the entrance arrangements for the keep.

The Keep

The keep was probably the first building to be erected by the Welsh at Dolforwyn in 1273. Initially free-standing, it would have dominated the site and later protected the main gateway to the castle. At this time, the 'square tower', as it is described in the 1322 survey, consisted of one large basement room with a timber ceiling, and one or more rooms above. It was entered at first-floor level via an external staircase and was served by latrines in the south-west corner of the building. Access to the basement was presumably via an internal wooden stair or ladder. In terms of size, it was the largest tower in all of the Welsh-built castles and the first floor no doubt served as a high-class chamber.

The keep was later modified by the English and the existing internal arrangements date principally from this time.

The Entrance and Interior
The English inserted the ground-floor doorway, but to do this, the Welsh-built stair had first to be cut back and made steeper. The two phases of the staircase can be distinguished in the surviving masonry. The new English doorway, distinguishable by its grey facing stones, still retains in its original position the lower iron hinge pin for the door.

Left: An artist's reconstruction of how the Welsh-built keep and the entrance arrangements to the castle may have looked in about 1276. The principal chamber would have occupied the first floor with a basement below, which was presumably accessible by an internal timber stair or ladder (Illustration by Chris Jones-Jenkins 2002).

Above: After 1277, an internal wall was inserted in the keep to create two rooms at ground-floor level. The doorway between the two appears to have been made reusing Roman stonework and incorporated an ingenious security arrangement, suggesting that the inner chamber was a strongroom such as a prison.

The north-west corner of the keep damaged during the 1277 siege was repaired with mortar stronger than the original. The original masonry has since collapsed and the repair has slumped outwards.

Inside, a thick partition wall was inserted, which divided the building in two. The outer room had its upper floor removed and would now have been a high single-storey chamber lit by a new window looking across the main courtyard. The inner room was entered via a doorway built of reused sandstone masonry. The tooling marks and hoist-holes suggest Roman work and these stones may have been brought from the auxiliary forts at Forden Gaer, near Montgomery, 6 miles (10km) to the east, or from Caersws, 8 miles (13km) to the west. The doorway itself was very well protected: it had a timber door that opened outwards into the larger room. Behind it was a drawbar, housed in a hole or slot within the thickness of the wall. There is no evidence of, or space for a second door, so the drawbar must have secured a different barrier — most likely a portcullis lowered from the room above. This double security and the contemporary thickening of the inner walls suggest that this room was used as a strongroom of some sort — perhaps a treasury or prison. The chamber above the inner room was

presumably served by the remodelled external staircase. The gap in the north wall has been caused by later root disturbance.

The 'benches' in the keep are an original constructional feature intended to strengthen the base of the tower on the two sides where it does not have an external battered sloping plinth.

The Exterior

Leave through the main entrance and turn right to examine the English repairs to the corners of the keep, which had been damaged by stone catapult balls in the 1277 siege (pp. 12–13).

The first (north-west) corner of the keep was repaired with an angled wall secured in lime mortar. The newly mortared stone was stronger than the sandy mortar of the original wall with the result that the new repair has tilted outwards as the older wall beneath it collapsed. The second (north-east) corner was repaired more carefully with the new wall built from foundation level, on rock, in squared grey stone secured with hard lime mortar. For added strength the corner was shaped

Right: Following the surrender of the castle to the English in 1277, the keep was divided by an internal wall and a new ground-floor entrance created. This artist's reconstruction suggests that a large chamber rising the full height of the building occupied most of the keep with a new large window overlooking the courtyard. The guardroom and adjacent store room were also added at this time (Illustration by Chris Jones-Jenkins 2002).

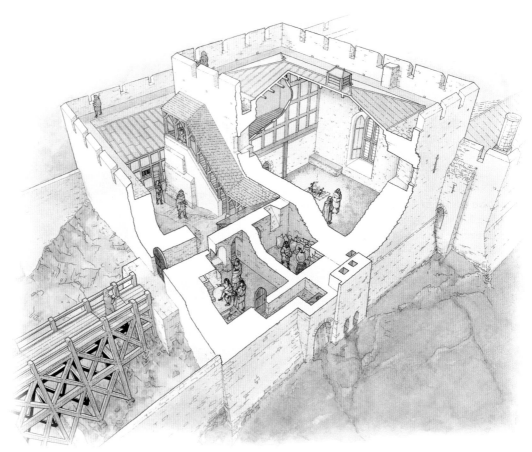

This curving stone drain indicates the position of a building which flanked the passage between the north curtain wall and keep.

to provide an angular turret; it also allowed wheeled traffic to pass safely for it was at the point where the passage into the courtyard was at its narrowest.

Although now empty of buildings, there would have been a half-timbered storage shed alongside the north curtain wall. Three features indicate its presence: a curving stone-lined drain, a window opening (now only visible as a few stones that formed the window arch set at an angle in the wall), and the vertical setting for the door frame fixed against the staircase wall. This staircase led to the wall-walk for soldiers to patrol.

The South Side of the Courtyard

Once inside the main courtyard, the rectangular plan of the castle can be readily appreciated. At the far end stands the Welsh-built circular tower and to the left its companion, the D-shaped tower. Unlike the square tower, both these towers project beyond the

line of the curtain wall. A rock-cut ditch, crossed by a bridge, divides the courtyard in two.

Lining the curtain walls on either side of the courtyard are the remains of domestic buildings, most of which date from the English occupation of the castle. Quarry pits along the south side showed where the construction of cellars had been interrupted and perhaps indicate that the Welsh builders did not have sufficient time to complete the internal fitting out of the castle.

The Bakehouse and the Brewhouse

The building against the south curtain, between the keep and the ditch, comprises two rooms that were separated by a timber partition — a bakehouse and a brewhouse — built alongside a stairway that gave access to the south curtain. Originally there were three separate doorways into the stairs, bakehouse and brewhouse, so that each could be accessed directly from the courtyard. Internal doorways also allowed access between all three areas.

The staircase with eleven surviving steps replaced a shorter stair; both led to the wall-walk on the south

Entrance →

curtain and probably also gave access to a latrine placed at the junction of the curtain wall and the keep. The later stair may also have led to a dry storage chamber over the ovens, perhaps to store flour.

In the bakehouse parts of three ovens can be identified. The largest, 11 feet (3m) in diameter, has a solid floor built of worn-out millstones and grindstones and would have been loaded at waist height. Part of the dome can be seen to the right of the sandstone jambs of the loading arch. A fire would have been lit on the oven floor and, when it was hot enough for baking, the ashes of the wood fire would have been raked out and the bread baked in the residual heat.

A similar side oven can be seen to the left; this also once had a floor made of grindstones. A third oven, with a flue beneath the stone baking floor, stood further to the left against the curtain wall (now rebuilt on the old footings, with the new masonry incorporating recessed pointing, a technique used throughout the site to distinguish new work from medieval). All these ovens were replacements for earlier smaller ovens.

There is now no visible evidence of the partition wall between the bakehouse and brewhouse or indeed of the brewing apparatus, but excavation recovered the impressions of two brewing vats, a roasting hearth and a steeping-trough. Alongside the south wall were large stones upon which the timber supports for the roof had stood at intervals of 16 feet (5m).

The Ditch, Bridge and South Gateway

A rock-cut ditch, crossed by a bridge corbelled over the narrowest part, divided the courtyard in two. The arch of the bridge remains intact with drain holes to protect the masonry core from waterlogging and to drain the roadway. At a later stage in the castle's history the bridge was doubled in width by building an additional arch on the north side.

At the southern end of the ditch, overlooking the Severn valley, are the remains of the Welsh-built south gateway, marked by two side buttresses that survive up to the springing of the arch. The gateway was closed by a double-leaf door secured with a wooden drawbar, housed in a slot 7 feet (2m) long. Originally, an access ramp — perhaps a ceremonial route of some sort — led from the gateway along the ditch towards the north tower,

but it was unfinished at the time of the English capture of the castle.

The ditch was abandoned and not dug any deeper or wider. The gateway was blocked by a wall, constructed in line with the outer wall face, with a drainage hole at its base. It echoed the sloping plinth of the adjoining earlier curtain and is best viewed from the exterior. At a late stage in the English occupation a second blocking wall was erected towards the back of the gateway; this, too, had a drain placed centrally at its base. After the castle was abandoned the space between these blocking walls was used as a dump for ornate pottery jugs, glass bowls, an ivory sphere, beads, jettons and food debris.

Part of the bakehouse built against the southern curtain, containing the remains of three ovens. The staircase, which gave access to the wall-walk, has been remodelled and the line of the original steps can be traced in the masonry.

This illustration from the Smithfield Decretals, *produced around 1330–40, shows bakers at work. Such a scene is likely to have been familiar at Dolforwyn (British Library, Royal Ms. 10 E IV, f. 145v).*

The southern half of the rock-cut ditch, which divides the courtyard in two, and the bridge that was corbelled to cross it at the narrowest point.

Below: The south gateway showing the various blocking arrangements.

Right: Llywelyn ab Iorwerth's great round tower at his castle at Dolbadarn, Gwynedd.

Below: The later thirteenth-century castle at Dinas Brân, near Llangollen, is almost contemporary with Dolforwyn and bears a striking resemblance to it in plan and location. Dinas Brân was probably built by Gruffudd ap Madog, prince of Powys Fadog and an ally of Llywelyn, about a decade earlier than Dolforwyn and the same masons may well have worked on both castles (RCAHMW).

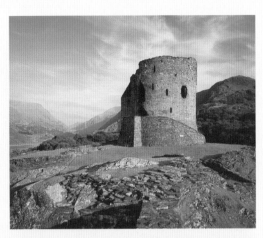

Comparative ground plans of castles of the Welsh princes

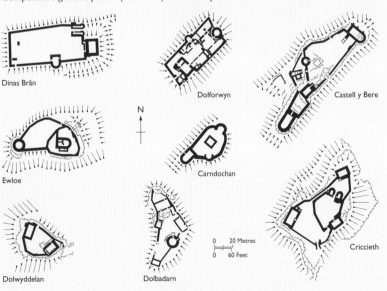

Dinas Brân

Ewloe

Dolwyddelan

Dolforwyn

N

Carndochan

Dolbadarn

0   20 Metres
0   60 Feet

Castell y Bere

Criccieth

Castles of the Welsh Princes

Before the Norman invasion Welsh rulers sometimes built stone fortifications on isolated craggy hilltops, often called '*dinas*', but their main preference was to live in undefended courts (*llysoedd*) and to rely on their bodyguard to protect them against attack or treachery. The practice of partible inheritance meant that estates were continually subdivided equally amongst all sons, with the result that only the most warlike ruler could amass sufficient land and resources to control a whole principality.

Matters changed, however, when the initial onslaught of the Norman barons against Wales proved devastating. Their use of mounted knights and the construction of earth-and-timber castles permitted them to seize and defend extensive territory in Wales. These early castles — a hitherto unknown phenomenon in Wales — took the form of either a motte-and-bailey or a ringwork and were soon imitated by the Welsh princes. A particularly good example survives at Tomen y Rhodwydd, built by Owain Gwynedd (d. 1170) in about 1150. The nature of the earthwork remains rarely makes it possible to distinguish Welsh from Norman construction. Nor is it possible to determine how Welsh castles were used at this time, since they do not seem to have replaced the role of the *llys*, or court, as the centre of the local district, or *commote* — unlike their Norman counterparts.

The Normans soon began to replace their earth-and-timber fortifications with stone towers and defensive enclosure walls, and by the late twelfth century the Welsh had adopted similar practices at a number of sites, including Tomen Castell at Dolwyddelan, Castell Aber Iâ or Deudraeth, and Cwm Prysor, near Trawsfynydd. The construction of these castles in isolated and naturally well defended positions may reflect the pre-existing Welsh preference for such locations.

Building in stone, however, required significant financial resources and labour, so it is not surprising that the most prolific Welsh castle builders were the two powerful thirteenth-century princes of

Gwynedd: Llywelyn ab Iorwerth (d. 1240) and
Llywelyn ap Gruffudd (d. 1282). Like their
compatriots in Powys and Deheubarth, they
continued to choose to build on rocky hilltops,
often commanding a valley or ford. Sometimes, as
at Castell y Bere in southern Gwynedd, it was a
spectacular outcrop, or, as at Criccieth, a coastal
peninsula. The shape of the hilltop dictated the
extent of the perimeter wall, which enclosed or
incorporated one or more of three preferred
designs of tower: circular, rectangular or D-shaped.
Frequently irregular in plan, the curtain linking the
towers was often of poor defensive quality, with
no thought given to flanking fire between towers.
Although most castles have strong rock-cut
ditches, gatehouses of any quality are rare,
resulting in a lack of any additional defensive
features at the main entrance. Exceptions to this
occur in the courtyard at Dolbadarn, where a
portcullis protected the doorway to the round
tower and, at Dolwyddelan, where a drawbridge
performed a similar function to a square tower.

There is no evidence of master masons,
and it seems that the design elements were
adopted from castles built by neighbouring
Anglo-Norman barons — with the exception
of D-shaped towers, which cannot be matched
in an English context. Llywelyn ab Iorwerth's
gatehouse at Criccieth, for example, has been
compared with that at Beeston built by Ranulf
de Blundeville (d. 1232), with whom he was
connected by the marriage of his daughter, Helen,
to John the Scot, Ranulf's nephew and heir.

Ultimately, the size and sophistication of
Welsh castles depended upon the importance
and resources of the builder and their need to
accommodate officials (constable, justiciar,
treasurer, gaoler) as well as a garrison and
household services. Labour, building materials
and food supplies would be drawn from the
immediate locality and financed by tribute paid
in respect of tenanted land. In return for their
services the local inhabitants would receive
protection. Specialist work by smiths, carpenters
and masons would be the responsibility of the
prince, and although rare, the survival of some
very fine sculptural fragments from Degannwy
and Castell y Bere is testimony to the
sophistication and status of these castles.

The Storeroom

Beyond the bridge and to the right of the
courtyard is a long storeroom. Excavation provided
very little evidence for its use apart from a
small clay-lined furnace and a large quantity of
nails. It was probably a half-timbered structure
built on a low stone wall at the present surviving
height. The socket for one vertical post (not
now visible) was found close to the round
tower. Originally this room had a wide doorway
and wooden steps down into it; late in the
castle's occupation the doorway was reduced
in size and stone steps were laid to allow easier
access into the room (now represented by
the modern metal steps). After the castle's
abandonment, this later entrance was narrowed
still further, perhaps to allow animals to be kept
within the room with a single hurdle closing
the new entrance.

The Round Tower

Built by Llywelyn ap Gruffudd, this strong circular
tower was initially free-standing before the adjoining
curtain wall was built. Similar to Welsh round towers
elsewhere, for example at Dolbadarn (Gwynedd),
the principal chamber — perhaps the prince's private
accommodation — was at first-floor level, accessed
by an external staircase. The whole of the tower
would have been rendered with mortar, and where
traces of the render survived, they have been
restored to give some impression of the original
appearance. Minor alterations followed during the
English occupation and in 1322 the round tower
was described as the armoury.

Soon after the round tower was completed
a low wall was erected north–south across the
courtyard in front of it, perhaps to provide a half-
timbered covered passageway. After the courtyard
ranges had been constructed during the English
occupation a second wall was built, which curved
around the tower and provided a covered passage
between the ground-floor entrance and the door
to the external stairway.

The outside stairway curved around the north-
west quadrant of the tower. With the exception of
two stone steps at the base, the remainder of the
stairway was constructed in timber. This led up to a

*This illustration of a blacksmith
is taken from a thirteenth-century
manuscript of the Welsh law book
of Hywel Dda. Such a craftsman
would have been important to the
castle community, making weapons,
locks and tools (National Library
of Wales, Peniarth Ms. 28, f. 6r).*

Entrance

Llywelyn ap Gruffudd's round tower sits astride the line of the curtain wall and dominates the eastern end of the castle. The curving line of the external timber stair can be seen to the left of the tower; there are just two stone steps at its base.

The interior of the round tower. A square hole, just to the right of the jagged break, probably housed the drawbar used to secure the door at the bottom of the external stair. Further to the right are two more square holes: these are putlog holes used to hold timber scaffolding.

defended platform in front of the entrance to the first-floor chamber, similar to those at Dolbadarn and Dolwyddelan, though both of these have stone-built steps. The stairway must also have given access to the upper rooms in the north range.

Today, the tower is entered by a ground-floor doorway, which seems to be an original, if unusual, feature. Inside, a central timber post would have supported the wooden ceiling above. Just to the right of a jagged break in the masonry there is a hole (at eye level), which is likely to have housed the drawbar used to secure the door at the foot of the external stair.

Two interesting features show how the tower was constructed. First, to the left (south) of the doorway the wall is stepped, which suggests that the tower was constructed over a number of seasons. Medieval masons could only use lime mortar in the frost-free summer months (May–September) and at the end of each season, incomplete walls would be left with stepped tops and covered to prevent weathering over the winter. This would also provide a good surface on which to resume work the following spring. Second, to the right of the drawbar hole are two deep holes that penetrate the walls. These are putlog holes intended for wooden scaffolding laid horizontally to support a platform, or masonry 'lift'. The inner wall surface is

badly eroded in this tower as a result of a Victorian excavation, which was not backfilled.

From outside the tower, overlooking the deep east ditch, you can best appreciate how the castle is perched on the highest point of the ridge. Beyond the large mound in front of you is another ditch, steep sided and flat-bottomed, which is likely to be English work. Also of English construction, to the south (right) of the tower, is the base of a latrine, which emptied down a rock-cut channel into the ditch.

To the north (left) the external details of the tower's construction are worthy of examination. A sloping plinth, built on a broad foundation course, rises to a protruding string course formed of single 'tile-stones', above which the wall face continues vertically. The outside of the external stair, however, has a vertical face throughout, as does the adjacent east curtain wall. But there is a marked contrast between the stairway and the curtain wall in the choice of stone and the type of masonry. The Welsh-built tower and stairway are constructed from thin dark grey-brown stone laid in the bedding plane, with long continuous courses and some levelling or packing. The curtain wall, however, is built of grey stones in squarish blocks with a few stones set on edge, which is characteristic of all the English repairs.

The North Side of the Courtyard

Unlike the buildings lining the south curtain, one section of those lining the north curtain was begun during the Welsh occupation of the castle and represents the only non-defensive structure dating from the period. During the Welsh phase, there was a long two-storey range in the north-east corner which, after 1277, was extended as far as the north tower. The English also constructed a well and built a new hall. During the English occupation there was a distinction between the south curtain buildings, which were utilitarian and supported the garrison, and those to the north, which were somewhat grander in nature and provided private accommodation. This distinction may also have been intended in the Welsh phase.

The two-storey north range is of Welsh construction roughly as far as the thin partition wall; the extension westwards towards the north tower dates from the English occupation.

Both phases of the building were terraced into the hillside necessitating the construction of a retaining wall between the courtyard and the free-standing south wall of this building, which still stands up to 8 feet (2.5m) high. The two doorways are part of the original construction suggesting that the ground floor may have been divided into two rooms from the outset. Three windows survive at ground-floor level.

Inside, details of the construction of the curtain wall are clear: there is an English repair at the north-east (right-hand) end and a 'bench' added along much of the northern wall to strengthen it. The main room has a stone-built pillar near the centre; this did not support a stone vault or the ceiling beams, but was the base for a fireplace at first-floor level, similar to those at Castell y Bere and Dryslwyn Castle. The large room above must have been impressive and may have served the Welsh prince as a hall. Note also the eastern window, which has an acutely angled internal splay to capture light from the courtyard without being blocked by the stairway to the round tower.

Moving westwards, there is the circular bowl of a corn-drying kiln, which occupied this area before the north range was built. Corn dryers operated using a low steady heat keeping the flames well away from the drying rack. From the shallow scoop in the earth floor where a wood fire was lit, a narrow flue drew the heat through a stone-built arch into the floor of the kiln bowl. From there the heat would rise to pass through the horsehair tray resting on the rim of the bowl. The corn or pulse to be dried or parched would be spread on this tray. If the fire was too fierce, then the tray would be burnt and the crop lost.

After the building had been extended, the western section was partitioned off by a low stone wall supporting a timber screen. This partition wall is likely to mark the extent of the original Welsh building. Beyond, there was a mortared surface over the natural rock and clay as far as the north tower that was probably connected with the tower's construction.

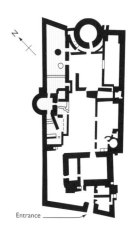

Below: The circular bowl of a corn-drying kiln, which pre-dates the construction of the north range.

Left: The thin partition wall in the foreground marks the approximate extent of the north range, as built by the Welsh. The building was later extended as far as the north tower. The stone-built pillar supported a hearth that probably served a hall at first-floor level (see reconstruction drawing, p. 35).

When the English took the castle their first action here was to construct a well to the south of the north tower, and it was probably at this time that the north range was extended. Next, they converted the east window in the north tower — that had originally overlooked the mortared yard — into a doorway leading into the north range. It was some time after these alterations that the partition wall was inserted. The western section of the building was found to be filled with blacksmithing debris, an anvil base, furnace bottoms and the clay-built shaft around the nozzle of a bellows — all of which was make-up material below a later earth floor.

The Well

The well was sunk through the northern end of the ditch that crossed the courtyard. Dug through solid rock to a depth of over 21 feet (6.5m), the well chamber was partly vaulted in stone and infilling walls were constructed to prevent the exposed rock face from fracturing and collapsing into the well shaft. It is still possible to identify the individual adze marks made by the quarrymen cutting into the rock. Side walls were also built to protect the north range and a narrow space to the west, which gave light to the north tower.

Holes in the side walls show the position of a wooden platform, just above the water level. It was from here that water would be drawn using some form of wooden winding mechanism, no doubt related to the wooden pulley wheel recovered from the well. Two staves from timber buckets were also found.

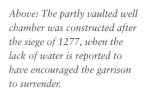

Above: The partly vaulted well chamber was constructed after the siege of 1277, when the lack of water is reported to have encouraged the garrison to surrender.

Right: An artist's reconstruction to show how the well may have been operated. The sockets for timbers to support the wooden platform can be seen in the side walls of the well chamber, just above the level of the water (Illustration by Chris Jones-Jenkins 2002).

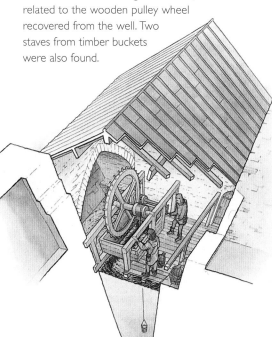

The North Tower

The north or D-shaped tower is Welsh in origin and was built at the mid-point of the north curtain with its curved face extending beyond the line of the perimeter wall. At this time, access to the basement level was via steps (still visible below the modern metal staircase) from an open area in the western end of the courtyard. These steps were blocked when the new hall was constructed at the higher courtyard level and a new doorway was created by breaking through a window into the north range. This now became the main entrance to the tower and reused some sandstone jambs, perhaps from the original doorway opposite (examples of which can be seen in the tower). There was also a window in the south wall of the tower.

There was no archaeological evidence of what rooms the tower contained or their purpose; nor is it mentioned specifically in the 1322 survey, though it is likely to have risen two floors above the basement and provided comfortable domestic accommodation. Some trace of white plaster survived on the inner wall surfaces and the outer face of the tower also retains extensive areas of white render. Although smaller than similar towers at Castell y Bere, it is comparable to the south tower at Dinas Brân, Llangollen, alongside which there was a hall range and an adjoining latrine (p. 30). Here, there is the base of a latrine outside at the eastern junction of the tower and curtain wall (best seen from outside).

The Hall

When the Welsh built the castle, this space was an open area with a surface of red clay. A doorway, or sally port, provided an exit from the castle at the north-west corner of the present building and stairs led down into the north tower.

However, when the English occupied the castle, they created a new room here — a hall, measuring 40 feet by 20 feet (12m x 6m), with a side aisle alongside the courtyard, and an inner chamber beyond — as indicated by the modern paving. The Welsh stair leading down into the north tower basement was covered over and reformed as the corner of the new building. The stair has now been excavated and consolidated for display and access, but it is, of course, of an earlier period and would not have been visible once the hall had been built. It is therefore important to understand that what is

visible on site today represents two different periods and would not have been seen together.

The original east end of the hall had collapsed into the well so modern masonry has been built over the surviving footings to show its former extent. The only entrance was at this end of the hall via a porch or lobby, now marked by slate slabs and the gap through the rebuilt masonry. The floor of the hall was made up of river cobbles with occasional pieces of worn-out grindstones and broken catapult balls, and there was a raised hearth made of siltstone, set on edge, which had been heavily burnt. The aisle on the left side was paved, its walls were plastered and it opened directly into the hall via an arcade of timber posts. There was evidence for a screen wall — marked by a wooden plank — set in a sill beam midway along the length of the aisle (see reconstruction drawing).

The floor level of the inner chamber was raised by 9 inches (0.25m) and paved. The walls retained traces of white plaster, but fragments decorated with red lines and patterns in black, blue and ochre were recovered during excavation, suggesting that both this room and the hall were ornate chambers. A window in the north wall, constructed where the earlier door or sally port had been, lit the inner room.

The Exterior of the Castle

From here you can either return to the car park or else make an anti-clockwise circuit of the exterior of the castle to view the towers, curtain walls, latrines and doorways.

The most impressive array of latrines can be seen on the south curtain, close to the keep. Here you can see a double latrine, with a single chute, that dates from the Welsh period and must have served soldiers stationed on the curtain wall. Later, it served the English guardroom (p. 26). Next, there is a double chute arrangement, which served the wall-walk during the English occupation of the castle, and then a single Welsh-built chute at the south-west corner of the keep. Another latrine was built later, by the English, close to the south-east corner of the keep.

Originally, massive ditches surrounded the castle, deeply cut across the ridge, but scarping back the hillside more steeply to north and south, though only the east ditch survives to any great depth. Note also the contrast between the long sides, which have a broad sloping plinth below the vertical wall face, and the short sides to the east and west, which are built up vertically, straight from the underlying rock.

Above: An artist's reconstruction of how the buildings on the north side of the courtyard may have looked in the fourteenth century following the construction of the well chamber, hall and remodelled north range. Here, the emphasis is on domestic comfort rather than military considerations (Illustration by Chris Jones-Jenkins 2002).

Chutes for latrines can be seen at several places on the exterior of the castle. This group is located on the south curtain and would have served the occupants of the keep and soldiers in the guardroom and on the wall-walk.

A Tour of Montgomery Castle

The town of Montgomery clusters around a pretty market square, overlooked by a red-brick town hall built in 1748. From here, it is possible to drive up to the castle, following the Cadw signs. Alternatively, there is a steeper road, unsuitable for cars, from beside the Dragon Hotel, or a woodland path uphill from just beyond the Old Bell Museum, where finds from the excavations at the castle and from its predecessor, Hen Domen, are on display. The first two roads bring the visitor to a car park, from where a path passes below a late seventeenth-century brick farmhouse and the castle outworks, to join the woodland path in front of the outer ditch, close to a circular dovecote.

From here, you can either follow the tour route suggested below, or explore the castle for yourself using the ground plan (inside back cover) and bird's-eye view (inside front cover).

The Outworks and Outer Ditch

The location of the castle is best appreciated from the top of the slope, above the dovecote. To the north and east, the site was protected by precipitous rocky slopes, and to the west by a steep valley separating it from the hillfort of Ffridd Faldwyn. Only the southern approach, along the ridge, would have been vulnerable. From here, an organized assault with siege engines would have been possible. The purpose of the outworks between the present farmhouse and the outer ditch was, therefore, to present a series of obstacles to would-be attackers from the south. With no direct route along the ridge, the medieval access road to the castle approached from the west, across what is now the farmyard to the west of the castle. The dam of the farmyard pond marks the site of a causeway (see reconstruction drawing p. 14).

The outworks themselves are made up of three elements — an outer D-shaped earth mound, originally revetted with masonry (behind the present farm); a rectangular barbican, with earth banks originally carrying palisades on its flanks; and a rock boss to the rear, which is immediately behind you. These works probably constitute the 'new bailey running from the road to Bedwin to the castle' recorded in 1229, and were most likely the work of Hubert de Burgh (p. 7). The area also saw active service in the seventeenth century when it was used by parliamentary troops both to conceal themselves before the 1644 attack on the castle and to house soldiers afterwards (pp. 21–23).

The dovecote contains brick fragments in its walls and is therefore probably contemporary with the early seventeenth-century Herbert house. The parliamentary garrison of 1644–49 cast musket shot here and debris from this, and other Civil War material, was found in and around the dovecote during excavation.

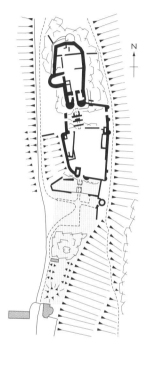

Left: The circular dovecote which probably dates from the early seventeenth century.

Opposite: The superb location of Montgomery Castle, high on a ridge overlooking the Severn valley, can probably be attributed to Hubert de Burgh, one of King Henry III's advisers who pointed out to him a site 'suitable for the erection of an impregnable castle'.

Right: One of the few surviving examples of a Welsh crwth, or bowed lyre (National Museums & Galleries of Wales).

Far right: A panel painting of around 1400 from the Chapter House at Westminster Abbey depicting an elder of the Apocalypse playing a bowed lyre (Courtesy of the Dean and Chapter of Westminster).

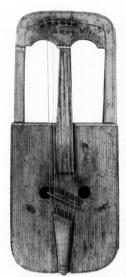

Musical Instruments

One group of finds illustrating an often overlooked aspect of life in medieval castles comprises four bone tuning pegs from a stringed musical instrument. These were found in a fourteenth-century context in the middle ward. They are probably from a bowed lyre, a type of traditional instrument found throughout much of western Europe and known in Wales as a *crwth*. Expert examination has shown that the pegs are not perforated like harp pegs, but notched at the top for horsehair strings of the kind which ethnographic parallels and medieval Welsh literary references alike show were used on the bowed lyre. Medieval illustrations of groups of musicians often show the harp and a bowed lyre in use side by side.

The rock-cut outer ditch and bridge abutment, above which stood the twin-towered outer gatehouse of the middle ward.

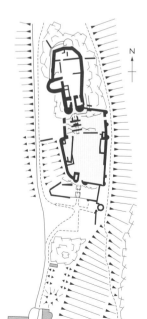

The Middle Ward

A modern timber bridge crosses the rock-cut outer ditch leading to the middle ward. Originally constructed in timber, the defences of the middle ward were not rebuilt in stone until 1251–53. The medieval arrangements of the internal buildings have largely been obliterated by the sixteenth- and seventeenth-century building activity of Bishop Rowland Lee and Edward Herbert, little of which survived the comprehensive demolition exercise at the close of the Civil War (pp. 20–23). However, it is reasonable to assume that the medieval accommodation would have included servants' and soldiers' lodgings, as well as service buildings to meet the needs of the wider castle community, as distinct from the king or the lord of the castle and his immediate associates housed in the inner ward.

The square-sectioned ditch, 45 feet (13.7m) wide and originally 22 feet (6.7m) deep, was largely filled with building rubble when the castle was demolished in 1649, but this has now been removed and the ditch is displayed at its latest medieval level. Below the outer gatehouse is a stone platform, part of the medieval bridge arrangements, on which the parliamentary engineers planted their petard on the night of 5 September 1644 (p. 22).

At the entrance to the middle ward are the slight remains of the two rounded towers of the outer gatehouse, built in 1251–53 together with the adjoining stone curtain wall (which is best seen from the outside; p. 7). To the east (right) the ground drops away and the curtain wall was built downslope from the rock ridge forming the crest of the ward. However, in the sixteenth century, the area between the curtain and the ridge was filled in by Bishop Rowland Lee to create a level building platform. It was necessary to remove this infill in order to conserve the curtain wall, and the ground is now displayed at its original medieval level.

Behind the east curtain, at the foot of the slope, is a fourteenth-century kiln house, where grain was dried after being harvested, and perhaps roasted to provide malt for brewing. The southern half of the building enclosed a masonry platform with a rectangular central flue. Clear traces of burning showed that a fire would have been lit in the mouth of the flue, the heat from which would have dried grain placed on a raised floor above. Paving in the centre formed a level floor from which the kiln could be stoked. The northern half of the building was of lighter construction, probably of timber on a stone foundation, and would have provided shelter and storage for the kiln workers and sacks of grain. There is a second, smaller unroofed kiln outside the north end of the kiln house.

To the south of the kiln house, several slightly built structures of similar date and construction were also excavated from where bone tuning pegs probably for a *crwth* — a traditional musical instrument known generally as a bowed lyre — were recovered. A series of jettons, or tokens for adding up accounts, was also discovered, suggesting that these structures may have been agricultural estate buildings.

During the sixteenth century, the west and south sides of the middle ward were lined with lodgings. The scant remains of the foundations of one sizeable building, perhaps the residence of Bishop Lee, can be seen inside the west curtain. The masonry-lined pit in the north-west corner of the ward indicates the site of its latrine. Bishop Lee's building was demolished when Edward Herbert's house was built in the seventeenth century (pp. 20–21). Traces of one range of the latter can be seen overlying it, including the only surviving part of its brickwork. The main range of the house was on the flat grassy area behind the south curtain, but nothing of this is now visible (see reconstruction drawing, p. 21).

Above: The remains of a fourteenth-century kiln house line the east curtain.

Left: A latrine pit in the north-west corner of the middle ward which probably served one of the domestic buildings erected by Bishop Rowland Lee in the sixteenth century.

The middle ward is now devoid of any standing buildings. However, the foundations in this view mark the site of buildings raised against the west curtain by Bishop Rowland Lee and Edward Herbert in the sixteenth and seventeenth centuries.

The Inner Ward

Constructed in stone from the outset, the buildings
of the inner ward were intended to house the king
and his immediate household when in residence, or
the lord of the castle and his followers — in effect,
a more compact version of the sets of apartments
found in other royal residences at this time. The main
apartments were in the large twin-towered inner
gatehouse, with a great chamber, private rooms and a
chapel. The castle well was in the adjacent D-shaped
tower, and the ward would have contained a timber
hall, with a timber bakehouse and kitchen. There may
have been another hall and chapel in the middle ward
for the wider castle community. The 1250 reference
to the inner ward and its buildings as *'le dunsun'*
(donjon), emphasizes their status as separate from
the remainder of the castle.

Inner Ditch

The rock-cut inner ditch, 45 feet (13.7m) wide
and 20 feet (6.1m) deep, with near vertical sides,
separates the middle ward from the inner ward to
the north, and is now spanned by a modern timber
bridge. The piers of two earlier, successive bridges
are visible on the broad flat floor of the ditch. The
medieval bridge was a three-span timber structure
resting on stone sole plates, the inner span being a
lifting bridge, which had to be renewed in 1250–51
and again in 1331 (see reconstruction drawing, p. 42).
This 'old bridge of Tymber' was 'somewhat perished'
in 1592–93 and Lord Herbert replaced it with a two-
span timber bridge resting on a central masonry pier.
The ditch was sealed off at either end by wing walls,
each containing a postern gate.

*Two pieces of sixteenth-century
armour excavated from the inner
ditch. The helmet (burgonet)
and defences for protecting the
arm (vambrace) are
likely to have been
captured from royalist
troops and discarded by
parliamentarian soldiers as
either obsolete or simply no longer
serviceable after the battle of
Montgomery in 1644 (The Old
Bell Museum, Montgomery).*

When the castle was demolished in 1649, the
ditch was filled with rubble, sealed beneath which
were some 600 pieces of Civil War armour (p. 22).
The majority of the pieces were of Italian or
Netherlandish style of about 1550 and decidedly out
of date by the time of the war. They included many
pieces of shoulder and arm defences (pauldrons and
vambraces); gorgets for the neck; laminated defences
for the thighs (tassets), fragments of a backplate and
the two halves of a two-piece helmet (burgonet).
One of the largest collections of excavated armour
on record, it was probably material captured
from the defeated royalist troops at the battle of
Montgomery. The parliamentarian soldiers may have
discarded some as obsolete, but probably kept the
still serviceable body armour (breasts and backs)
and helmets (save for the single broken example),
which are conspicuously missing from the collection.

The Inner Gatehouse

The internal arrangement of the gatehouse can
be deduced from the 1592–93 survey and other
documentary sources, as well as from the existing
remains (see reconstruction drawing, p. 42). Like
the rest of the inner ward, the gatehouse was built
of metamorphosed greenstone rubble, dug from
the castle ditches, with dressings of red sandstone
ashlar from near Shrewsbury, many blocks of which
carry masons' marks. Allocated to individual masons,
the marks could be used to identify their work —
often paid as piecework — and to act as a form of
quality control so that any faulty work could be
traced to its source.

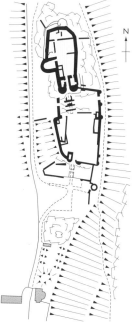

*Left: The inner ditch, which
separates the middle and inner
wards, was sealed at both ends
by a wing wall, each containing
a postern. Piers in the bottom
of the ditch indicate two earlier
bridge arrangements.*

*Opposite: Although ruinous,
following deliberate despoliation
at the end of the Civil War, the well
tower (left) and west wall of the
inner gatehouse (centre) still stand
to a height of more than 50 feet
(15m) and retain sufficient detail
to suggest the remarkable quality
of the inner ward buildings.*

An artist's reconstruction of the inner gatehouse as it may have looked in the later thirteenth century. The picture is cutaway to show the internal arrangements of the chambers above the gate-passage and the timber-built chapel and gallery (Illustration by Chris Jones-Jenkins 2002).

Below: The twin towers flanking the gate-passage to the inner ward are now reduced to their solid foundations. Each tower was three-quarters round with a rectangular chamber behind.

The gatehouse consists of a gate-passage, 7 feet (2m) wide, flanked by a pair of three-quarter-round towers, solid in their lower parts and with a rectangular room behind each tower. As the most vulnerable part of the castle, the gate-passage was protected by a portcullis, the grooves of which are visible, and two pairs of heavy double doors — one at each end of the passage. A most unusual source of information suggests that there might also have been a 'murder hole' — a hole through which projectiles could be dropped on attackers — namely, the evidence given at the inquest into the death of Maud Vras, on New Year's Day 1288.

It appears that Maud Vras, a widow, toiled up from the town to recover a kettle that she had lent to the assistant constable of the castle, William of St Albans. As she stood at the entrance to the inner gatehouse, under the portcullis, William was in the room over the gate, trying on a new cloak. Apparently, whilst in the process of wrestling with the garment, it unfortunately caught on a stone (possibly a stone catapult ball) which fell through the middle of the portcullis, onto Maud's head, causing her to die the same day. Whether the stone rolled through the portcullis slot, or through a murder hole, which may be more likely, will never be known. Whatever the exact explanation, William of St Albans was held in custody pending further enquiries, but a jury found him not guilty of a premeditated felony and he was eventually pardoned. The verdict returned was 'death by misadventure'.

The sides of the gate-passage were formed of arched recesses, with bench-like features below, and four square cupboard-like niches in the angles. These originally had wooden doors or grilles, and may have been lamp niches to light the otherwise dark gate-passage. There was originally no access from the gate-passage to the ground-floor rooms on each side, the door on the left being cut through the earlier masonry in the late thirteenth or fourteenth century. It leads to an unlit 'darke chamber', which probably served as a storeroom or prison and could originally only be accessed from the room above by ladder. Opposite is a guardroom,

which was entered from the inner ward by a doorway of finely dressed red sandstone ashlar, equipped with a drawbar housed within the thickness of the wall. The room was lit by a slit window, overlooking the town, and it was from this chamber that the drawbar for the door at the front of the gatehouse was worked. The purpose of a cupboard-like feature in the end wall is uncertain; it may be another lamp niche, or a means of communication between the porter's lodge and those working the portcullis on the floor above.

Only the west wall of the gatehouse survives above first-floor level, but the now missing upper floors of the gatehouse are described in the 1592–93 survey. There was a 'lardge payre' of timber stairs to the left (west) of the entrance to the inner ward, leading to a covered gallery that ran between the well tower and the gatehouse, with an oriel, or landing, lit by a large window, that gave access to 'a lyttle chappell of tymber … standinge upon ii postes right over thentringe in of the same gate' (see reconstruction drawing).

Rows of beam holes for the first and second floors can be seen, together with a gap for a tall window, to the left of which was a latrine chamber. The slot for its wooden seat can be seen in the

Above: The west side of the gatehouse passage, with one of the four niches in the foreground. A door jamb and portcullis slot can be seen beyond.

Below left: The inner ward looking towards the back of the gatehouse — the site of the 'lyttle chappell of tymber'.

Below: An artist's reconstruction of the chapel that was recorded in the survey of 1592–93. It is unclear when this arrangement was adopted but it may date from the mid-thirteenth century. The first-floor timber gallery would have connected the gatehouse chambers with those of the well tower. (Illustration by Chris Jones-Jenkins 2002).

Right: Part of the north curtain wall of the castle at Degannwy, overlooking the Conwy estuary. Originally a Welsh stronghold, Henry III spent large sums on rebuilding the castle between 1245 and 1253, following its destruction by Dafydd ap Llywelyn in 1241.

Above: Edward I's magnificent fortress at Caernarfon, begun in 1283. The colour-banded walls and polygonal towers are reminiscent of the Roman Imperial walls at Constantinople and may have been intended as a conscious display of the king's power.

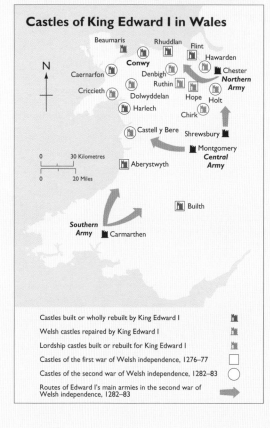

Castles of King Edward I in Wales

N

Beaumaris
Rhuddlan
Flint
Hawarden
Conwy
Caernarfon
Denbigh
Chester
Northern Army
Criccieth
Ruthin
Dolwyddelan
Hope
Holt
Harlech
Chirk
Castell y Bere
Shrewsbury
Montgomery
Central Army
Aberystwyth

0   30 Kilometres
0   20 Miles

Builth

Southern Army
Carmarthen

Castles built or wholly rebuilt by King Edward I
Welsh castles repaired by King Edward I
Lordship castles built or rebuilt for King Edward I
Castles of the first war of Welsh independence, 1276–77
Castles of the second war of Welsh independence, 1282–83
Routes of Edward I's main armies in the second war of Welsh independence, 1282–83

Royal Castles in Wales

From William the Conqueror's work at the Tower of London to Edward I's magnificent castles in north Wales and beyond, the medieval kings of England were at the forefront of medieval military architecture. They could command money and labour in sufficient quantity to build, at times, on an unprecedented scale. The costs of these works were entered each year in the royal accounts and in many cases these records, long preserved in the Tower of London, are now in The National Archives. They form one of the most important sources for the study of medieval royal castles.

Royal castle building in Wales, however, was not common until the later thirteenth century for, unlike England, the conquest of Wales was left to a handful of Norman barons, who carved out large lordships on the borders, over which they had almost unlimited control. Here, they built castles, imitated by the Welsh (p. 30), but they had little interference from the king. Nevertheless, castles occasionally reverted to the Crown and some royal building works are recorded during this period. Despite a chequered history, Carmarthen served as a royal castle from the reign of Henry I onwards and during the reign of Henry II various building works were undertaken at a few castles in Glamorgan and Monmouthshire. But it was not until 1223, with the construction of Montgomery, that a new royal castle was built in Wales on an entirely fresh site.

The royal accounts for Montgomery record the annual costs between 1223 and 1233, and show how work was progressing. The overall figure, however, includes the wages of the garrison, so that the total cost of building the castle cannot be worked out. Nor is there any indication of which parts of the castle were being built in any particular year, though later accounts do make more specific references. As part of a more aggressive policy towards Wales, Henry III also refortified the castles at Builth, Painscastle, Dyserth and Degannwy, but these were to pale into insignificance when compared with the mighty fortresses erected by his son, Edward I.

Edward's conquest of Wales, between 1277 and 1283, coincided with the high water mark of medieval castle building and gave him both the resources and the reason to build a series of massive castles to control his new territories and so prevent the heartland of Gwynedd from ever again becoming a focal point for Welsh resistance. Between 1277 and 1295 the king embarked on building no less than eight new castles (see map) — employing the most up-to-date techniques of military architecture — and he was involved in the construction or refurbishment of another nine.

Up to 3,000 masons, carpenters, labourers and ditch diggers were recruited throughout the realm, and sent, sometimes under armed guard, to the king's new works in north Wales. In terms of the organization of transport, the recruitment of the workforce and the purchase of material, this was indeed a masterpiece of logistical planning. Much of the work was supervised by Master James of St George, the master of the king's works in Wales, who had previously been employed by the counts of Savoy, and had long experience of castle building before transferring to Edward's service in about 1278.

Each of Edward's new castles was perfectly adapted to its carefully chosen location — always within easy access of the sea — and round towers, twin-towered gatehouses and concentric curtain walls combined to provide extensive, comfortable accommodation within a well-nigh impregnable fortress. Caernarfon, however, was the exception with its banded polygonal towers. These consciously recalled the Roman Imperial walls of Constantinople and it was at Caernarfon that, according to tradition, the first English prince of Wales was born in 1284 — the future Edward II.

Although royal castles in Wales were maintained and repaired when necessary — especially at times of national crisis, such as during the revolt of Owain Glyn Dŵr (1400–06/7), the Wars of the Roses (1455–85) and the Civil War (1642–48) — building work never again attained the scale or impact of the Edwardian strongholds. Four of these 'consummate masterpieces of medieval military architecture' — Beaumaris, Caernarfon, Conwy and Harlech — have since been recognized as World Heritage Sites.

masonry and the chute is visible externally. The gatehouse may have had a third floor, which has since been destroyed. The portcullis was probably operated from the floor above the gate-passage, the remainder of which may have served as a great chamber — the 'knight's chamber near the chapel' in the 1250 survey. Here, members of the household and those on business at the castle would be admitted. The floor above, however, probably contained the private apartments of the lord of the castle.

The Well Tower

Beyond the gatehouse, to the left, a remodelled doorway containing jambs of reused finely carved stone leads into the ground floor of the well tower. When the castle was first begun in 1223, twenty miners from the Forest of Dean sank a vertical shaft here to a depth of about 210 feet (64m), from the top of the castle rock to a spot below where damp green vegetation suggested the presence of water. Hubert de Burgh, the king's adviser at Montgomery and a veteran of two long castle sieges, knew the significance of water to a besieged garrison; some fifty years later the Welsh garrison at Dolforwyn had to surrender due to a water shortage (p. 12).

The well tower projects out from the west face of the castle over the sloping rock. In order to create a level platform for the ground floor, rubble was

The 1250 survey of the castle mentions the 'knight's chamber near the chapel', and also records the presence of 'the old hall within the donjon' built of crucks (furcis) (The National Archives: PRO, SC 1/3, f. 153).

Left: The well tower, so named because it housed the castle's water supply.

Below: Finely carved stone was reused for the jambs of the remodelled ground-floor doorway into the well tower.

A timber bucket, complete with suspension chain, recovered from the well shaft at Montgomery (The Old Bell Museum, Montgomery).

dumped against this sloping rock face and the well shaft dug through it. The top 6 feet (1.7m) of the well was circular and built of mortared sandstone blocks; below this level it continued as a square rock-cut shaft.

This method of construction led to structural problems, for within ten years it was necessary to spend £86 on repairing the tower. It evidently continued to give trouble, for in 1310 the well tower was 'on the point of falling to pieces' and was largely taken down and rebuilt some time later. In its rebuilt form, the well chamber was on the ground floor, with a room described in 1592–93 as a 'fair dining chamber' above. Only the north wall of this room and the jamb of one window survive. The deep vertical rift marks the junction between the original thirteenth-century structure and the repair work of the fourteenth century.

The well itself was excavated between 1973 and 1974. This revealed that it had been filled with stone rubble to a depth of 178 feet (54m), perhaps deliberately, since an open shaft would have been very dangerous. Below the rubble was a thick layer of wet black mud, which contained an iron-bound, barrel-like well bucket, still with its suspension hook; a series of other wooden vessels; a leather pistol holster of the Civil War period; shoes and cobbler's waste; and other organic material. There was also a large quantity of animal bone, including eleven dogs, suggesting that the well — by now an open shaft amidst tree-covered ruins — was a convenient place for the disposal of dead animals. The lowest — and earliest — deposits consisted of fine grey shale that had eroded off the sides of the well in medieval times.

The Buildings of the Inner Ward

Little survives of the earlier medieval arrangements within the inner ward, though there must have been a variety of lodging and service buildings to serve the king's household. When the north curtain wall was built in 1224–27, the sloping rock face inside it was levelled up with building debris and occupation material to create a flat surface. The debris included masons' chippings, spoilt ashlar blocks and spreads of mortar, interleaved with layers of black soil containing bones of food animals, much pottery and a coin of Henry III, which was lost between 1216 and 1225 (and coincides with the documentary evidence for the date of the castle).

The only building which may survive from this early phase consists of two east–west walls, which are more substantial than those of the various later lodgings. One now forms the south wall of the brewhouse, the other, which is incomplete, is opposite the north wall of the well tower. These could be the foundations of a timber-framed hall, which would have created a courtyard in the southern part of the ward, between the hall and the gatehouse. In 1250, the 'old hall within the donjon' (inner ward) was repaired with arched timbers (*furcis* — crucks), lengthened by about 6 feet (1.7m) and roofed with wooden shingles. Associated with it were a timber bakehouse and kitchen, perhaps on the site of their successors.

Sometime after 1280 (p. 14), an L-shaped block containing a kitchen and brewhouse was built in the north-west angle of the ward. The kitchen, beyond the well tower, has a massive circular oven at one end, the floor of which was built of thin stone slabs set on edge, covered by a layer of clay-brick pads, to resist the effects of fire. Originally, there would have been

Right: The inner ward would have contained a range of service buildings and lodgings that would have been modified over time to meet the needs of the castle's occupants. The earliest structure, which is represented by the two east–west walls seen here, may have been a hall and is believed to date from when the castle was established in 1223.

Far right: Part of the kitchen block, built against the west curtain, adjacent to the well tower.

a domed masonry superstructure and chimney (which was 'decaed and fallen downe' in 1592–93). The food would have been prepared on a long wooden table running the length of the kitchen.

Next to this, against the north curtain, is the brewhouse for beer, entered down a shallow flight of three semicircular steps. Barley would have been soaked in the rectangular tank against the north curtain, then spread on the paved area to the west to germinate, roasted in the small oven and ground with a handmill. The remaining processes involved running liquids between tanks for fermenting and boiling, and this was done on the upper floor, so that the liquids could be transferred between the tanks by gravity. East of the brewhouse, a series of drains carried away the waste liquids and discharged through the curtain.

In its final phase, the inner ward was lined with a series of lodgings ranged around the curtain wall. These were two-storey timber-framed structures set on light foundation walls of rubble masonry. A typical example can be found behind the entrance to the inner ward, between the gatehouse and the well tower. Its foundations include a large reused medieval architectural fragment with elaborate mouldings. The lodgings elsewhere in the ward were less well preserved: on the east side, only a rectangular fireplace survived. Some of the lodgings were probably built by Bishop Rowland Lee between about 1537 and 1539, and would have housed officials and members of his household, as befitted a major Tudor magnate and administrator, though other buildings may be later. A third small L-shaped lodging block and stable overlay the later medieval kitchen and brewhouse.

The Exterior of the Castle

A walk around the exterior of the castle walls fully repays the effort. Visitors will, in any case, need to retrace their steps to the area outside the outer ditch. From here, a path leads past the dovecote to the outer face of the east curtain of the middle ward. Its main features are four shallow semi-circular turrets, which could have supported projecting defensive wooden superstructures, such as those seen on a number of continental castles and town walls. With the exception of the second turret, this part of the middle ward defences appears to have been raised in one phase, between 1251 and 1253. The second turret, which

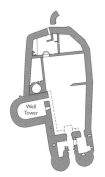

Early–mid-thirteenth century   *Late thirteenth–fourteenth century*   *Sixteenth century*

Servants preparing food on wooden tables are shown in this detail from the fourteenth-century Luttrell Psalter. *No doubt similar activities took place in the kitchen at Montgomery (British Library, Additional Ms. 42130, f. 207v).*

The brewhouse which occupied the north end of the inner ward from the late thirteenth century until it was remodelled in the sixteenth century.

Part of the east curtain wall of the middle ward with two of the rounded turrets, which may have supported wooden fighting platforms.

The remains of the large round tower at the north end of the castle.

stands on a small plinth and is not bonded into the curtain wall, is believed to date from the time that the well tower was reconstructed, sometime in the fourteenth century. Two turrets flank the postern gate of the inner ditch, on the floor of which can be seen the foundations of the three-span medieval timber bridge and the central pier of its seventeenth-century successor.

Beyond the postern gate, the curtain walls of the inner ward stand atop the castle rock, with a precipitous wooded slope above the town on the right. At the north-east angle is another postern gate, blocked up when the brewhouse was built inside the curtain. The foundations of a thirteenth-century semi-circular tower, which was later demolished, are visible on the north face of the castle. There is a small door in its western flank and from here the curtain wall curves round to the well tower. Note the fine latrine chute in this stretch of curtain. Another postern gate leads into the bottom of the inner ditch, beyond which the slight remains of the western curtain wall can be seen above the ditch and rock slope.

A fine latrine chute on the west curtain wall of the inner ward.

Further Reading

Acknowledgements Cadw and the authors would like to thank Professor Rees Davies and Professor Ralph Griffiths for their assistance with the text.

General Reading

R. Avent, *Castles of the Princes of Gwynedd* (Cardiff 1983).

H. M. Colvin, general editor, *The History of the King's Works*, vol. II (London 1963), 739–42.

R. R. Davies, *Conquest, Coexistence and Change: Wales 1063–1415* (Oxford 1987); reprinted in paperback as, *The Age of Conquest: Wales 1063–1415* (Oxford 1991).

P. Gaunt, *A Nation Under Siege: The Civil War in Wales 1642–48* (London 1991).

C. Hopkinson and M. Speight, *The Mortimers, Lords of the March* (Logaston 2002).

J. E. Lloyd, *A History of Wales*, vols I and II, third edition (London 1939).

J. B. Smith, *Llywelyn ap Gruffudd* (Cardiff 1998).

M. W. Thompson, *The Decline of the Castle* (Cambridge 1987).

G. Williams, *Recovery, Reorientation and Reformation: Wales c. 1415–1642* (Oxford 1987); reprinted in paperback as *Renewal and Reformation: Wales c. 1415–1642* (Oxford 1993).

Dolforwyn Castle

L. A. S. Butler, 'Dolforwyn Castle, Montgomery, Powys: First Report, The Excavations 1981–1986', *Archaeologia Cambrensis* **138** (1989), 78–98.

L. A. S. Butler, 'Dolforwyn Castle, Montgomery, Powys: Second Report, The Excavations 1987–1994', *Archaeologia Cambrensis* **144** (1995), 133–203.

L. A. S. Butler, 'Dolforwyn Castle: Prospect and Retrospect', in J. R. Kenyon and K. O'Conor, editors, *The Medieval Castle in Ireland and Wales* (Dublin 2003), 149–162.

Montgomery Castle

P. Barker and R. Higham, *Hen Domen, Montgomery: A Timber Castle on the English–Welsh Border*, vol. I (London 1982).

P. Gaunt, '"One of the Goodliest and Strongest Places that I Ever Looked Upon": Montgomery and the Civil War' in Diana Dunn, editor, *War and Society in Medieval and Early Modern Britain* (Liverpool 2000), 180–203.

R. Higham and P. Barker, *Hen Domen, Montgomery: A Timber Castle on the English–Welsh Border* (Exeter 2000).

J. K. Knight, 'Excavations at Montgomery Castle: Part I. The Documentary Evidence, Structures and Excavated Features' *Archaeologia Cambrensis* **141** (1992), 97–180.

J. K. Knight, 'Excavations at Montgomery Castle: Part II. The Finds', *Archaeologia Cambrensis* **142** (1993), 182–242.

J. K. Knight, 'Excavations at Montgomery Castle: Part III. The Finds (other than Metalwork)', *Archaeologia Cambrensis* **143** (1994), 139–203.

J. M. Lewis, 'The Excavation of the "New Building" at Montgomery Castle', *Archaeologia Cambrensis* **117** (1968), 127–56.

J. D. K. Lloyd, 'Montgomery Castle and the Herberts', *Archaeologia Cambrensis* **104** (1955), 52–64.

J. D. K. Lloyd, 'The "New Building" at Montgomery Castle', *Archaeologia Cambrensis* **114** (1965), 60–68.

J. D. K. Lloyd and J. K. Knight, *Montgomery Castle*, second edition (Cardiff 1981).

A. J. Taylor, 'An Incident at Montgomery Castle on New Year's Day, 1288', *Archaeologia Cambrensis* **116** (1967), 159–64.